Endorsements for
The Truth About Sex Trafficking

"This book is exceptional! Very well thought out and informative. It is a must read for parents and all those working in the medical or social service field. As an adoptive mother and foster parent to children that have been trafficked, I wish I had had this information when my journey began. The book is easy to read, with just enough story line to keep you interested. I have read many articles and books on human trafficking and this is hands down the best I have read. It gives a real picture of not only what trafficking is but how to interact and show compassion to those that have been trafficked."

Melody Higgins, LMSW, Children's of Alabama

"As a licensed professional counselor, I read this book looking to see what new thing I could learn. Ms. Patterson's work did not disappoint. The stories are absolutely heartbreaking while eye opening at the same time."

Cherie May Edwards, LPC-S

"The author approaches the subject matter with an open and non-judgmental mindset. She doesn't shy away from this uncomfortable topic. People often only hear or read about the statistics of sex crimes. The victim is usually a nameless shadowy silhouette next to the news reporter's face. Rarely do people have an opportunity to hear from the victim; their experiences and how they escaped. This book talks about the immeasurable resources that law enforcement and anti-sex trafficking advocates use to help the victims and survivors. The book also allows the reader to clearly understand how anyone can become a victim of sex trafficking. *The Truth About Sex Trafficking* removes the secure feeling of 'It only happens to other people or *those kinds* of people.' This book lifts the facade of safety and allows us to see the ugliness that may exist right under our noses. Only in the light of this brutal honesty can we, as a society, begin to identify and help victims who are in need."

Jennifer L. Anderson, Crime Laboratory Technician, Crime Scene Unit, Baltimore City Police Department; M.S. in Skeletal Trauma Analysis and Medicolegal Death Investigation

"Melanie K. Patterson fully explores the multifaceted and often misunderstood subject of human trafficking. From defining its many, often tangled layers, to explaining laws and resources, *The Truth About Sex Trafficking* is a must read for anyone who knows of the term 'human trafficking,' but doesn't clearly understand it. It should also be required reading for anyone who will be working in the many fields that will potentially bring them into contact with a trafficked individual."

Donna Funderburke McKinley, Founder, McKinley Reports

THE TRUTH ABOUT SEX TRAFFICKING

The Truth About Sex Trafficking

A Survivor's Experience and What It Means for All of Us

MELANIE K. PATTERSON

Forged In Words Books

Forged In Words Books

Second Printing, 2022

ISBN: 978-0-578-28548-1
eBook ISBN: 978-0-578-28549-8

Cover design by Romana Bovan

Printed in the United States of America

To all victims and survivors, and to all who help them.

CONTENTS

X - CONTENTS

Author's Note

In this book, human sex traffickers and buyers are usually referred to as males, and trafficking victims are usually referred to as females. Statistically, most traffickers and buyers are men. Adult victims are most often women. But in fact, traffickers, buyers and victims can be of any gender. I use male and female pronouns to keep the writing simpler, and transgender when it applies. This is not meant to minimize the existence of victims, traffickers and buyers that are not in the majority, gender-wise.

Also, many anti-sex trafficking advocates steer away from using the word "victim," preferring to say "survivor," or "active survivor" if the person is still being trafficked. Within their organizations, they use survivor instead of victim because they say it is more empowering. In this book, however, I do use both terms, not as a sign of disrespect, but because legislation, government reports, websites and some advocates continue to use the term victim. In this book, victim refers to people who are still being trafficked and survivor refers to people who are no longer being trafficked.

Other terminology considerations are the words "trafficker" and "pimp." Some sources use the words interchangeably. This book takes that approach. Amy Wagar, an advocate for Worthy[2] (Worthy Squared) and a trainer for the Child Trafficking Solutions Project, explains that trafficker is a legal or official term, and pimp is a street term.

Some people in this book use the term "john," which means a person who pays for sex. Also, the term "turning tricks" refers to performing sex acts for money.

Introduction

This book follows the story of Angela. That's not her real name, but she is a real human sex trafficking survivor who is unbelievably brave. She survived the terror of being trafficked and today she's married with three kids, has a master's degree and has helped many other survivors. Angela agreed to talk about her experience for a simple reason—she wants to help others. She is a true hero.

WHY?

When friends and family found out I was writing this book, the most typical questions I received were variations of, "Why?"

Why would you write about that?

What made you want to write about something so sad? So depressing? So dark?

Why would you write about something so dangerous—won't the traffickers come after you?

People also ask whether something like this ever happened to me. It didn't.

The book started as an assignment in 2012. I was editor of a small newspaper, The North Jefferson News in Gardendale, Alabama. On Wednesdays, we covered the weekly Gardendale Rotary Club luncheon. It was a routine assignment with the lure of a free lunch.

Most reporters I know are indifferent about covering civic club meetings. Just part of the job, often mundane, but important in their own right. Sometimes the speakers are good, sometimes not.

At every newspaper I ever worked for, the reporters were mostly excited about the food. "Who's catering?" held more weight than, "Who's speaking?"

Then came the civic club meeting that changed everything. I don't even remember what I had for lunch that day. I don't remember the name of the speaker, but her message disturbed me for years. The woman worked at The WellHouse, an organization in Birmingham, Alabama, that helps sex trafficking survivors recover from their trauma and build a new life. The speaker at the luncheon told us that Interstate 20/59 that runs east and west through Birmingham is one of the major corridors of human trafficking in the United States. I was shocked—I use that interstate all the time.

The woman told us that she had driven one of her clients through Birmingham, where the client pointed out numerous buildings where she had been sold for sex. Some of them were buildings where nice, professional people worked—not the sort of people I expected to go to a website and order a woman or child to be delivered to them for sex. This happened fifteen minutes from where I worked in Gardendale every day.

The speaker had put a name to something that happened to a friend many years ago. When my friend was fifteen years old, her mother couldn't cover the rent one month. The mother made an arrangement with the landlord: she allowed him to rape her daughter in exchange for the rent. I didn't realize until that day at the Rotary Club meeting that my friend's mother had trafficked her. Familial trafficking is common in the United States.

As the years passed, the speaker's words would not leave me alone. I would be reminded of them by a song or a billboard or by nothing at all. But for a long time, I mostly ignored the tragedy of human trafficking as something too hard to think about.

I think the real answer to "why" came in February 2022. A good friend called and said, "Hey, are you still working on that sex trafficking book?" I said yes, and she told me about a long text message she had received from a young woman I will call Sarah. Sarah texted my friend that she was being drugged and trafficked. "I don't understand," my friend told me. "I thought being trafficked meant that somebody takes you somewhere else. But she's still here." I told my friend that people can be trafficked from their own homes by family members or friends. I also told her that it's common for traffickers to force their victims to use drugs. I could hear the amazement in her voice as she realized that Sarah really was being trafficked by someone she knew. I sent my friend the information to get help.

Even though the book had not yet been released, it helped my friend learn more about sex trafficking. Even better, Sarah reached out for help, and received it. She was placed in a residential facility that helps sex trafficking survivors heal. A few days after her first text to my friend, she sent another text: "I'm on my way to a new life."

That's the best answer I could ever give about why I'm writing this book.

APPROACH

When the time came to start working on the book, one of the women I interviewed, Amy Wagar, asked what my angle was. "Political?" she asked. "Religious?" I assured her that I was taking neither of those approaches.

Wagar pointed out something that I later realized applies to my journey regarding this book. She said people often want to get involved in the fight against human trafficking with idealistic views. They want to fix the entire problem on the first day. But the volunteers for the organization she led at the time, Trafficking Hope, are required to go through extensive training before their feet ever touch the streets. "Most people come in just like I was—'I'm ready to go start beating bad guys up and rescuing people. Let's just do this,'" Wagar said, laughing. "A lot of our team comes in like that, and they're not ready to go out and be effective until their heart is in the right place."

That was true for me, too. The knowledge and heartbreak about human trafficking victims came in 2012 when I heard the woman from The WellHouse. The idea to write a book about it came in 2018. I started interviewing people in 2020. I quit my full-time job and began writing the book in September 2021. It took that long for my heart to get in the right place.

When the time came to finally get started, I wasn't sure how to go about it. Nobody who works in the field of human sex trafficking knew me. Why would they talk to me? I knew they would be extremely protective of their clients, and rightfully so. They had no reason to trust me.

I sent out a few emails. Amazingly, a couple of people responded. Quite a few didn't. The first person I interviewed for this book was Carolyn Potter, CEO of The WellHouse. It was the same organization I had written the newspaper article about eight years earlier. The next person was Kathy Wilson, Cofounder of the Cullman County (Alabama) Human Trafficking Task Force.

Both women kindly suggested other people I should talk to. Mostly, they recommended the same people. I shamelessly name-dropped when I sent out the next batch of emails. "Dear So-and-so, I've interviewed Carolyn and Kathy for a book I'm working on and they said I should talk to you. See, I'm not a horrible person, I've been vetted by people you trust!" I didn't write those exact words, but I was hoping they would read between the lines.

With much grace and kindness, people did agree to talk with me. Potter and Wilson got it started, the people they recommended suggested other folks, and so it went. One interview at a time, the information in the following pages seemed to gather itself. I got additional valuable information when I attended an online anti-trafficking conference hosted by the National Trafficking Sheltered Alliance, researched numerous anti-trafficking websites, and read some great books. (See the Resources chapter for recommendations for further reading and research.)

PURPOSE

One of my biggest worries with this book is being accused of re-exploiting sex trafficking victims and survivors. My first idea was to track down as many survivors as possible and tell their stories.

I learned better.

After some research, I now know that survivors can be re-traumatized by telling their stories, especially if they haven't received trauma counseling and other professional help. I learned about survivors who had been re-exploited by sensational media reports.

So, instead of talking to many survivors, I decided to use one woman's story as a thread throughout the book to connect all of the topics covered. Angela assured me that she was comfortable telling me about her experience. A woman of strong faith, she prayed about it and decided she was ready. She has been out of trafficking for more than twenty years, and has received intense counseling. She has even helped other victims through her work in Christian ministries. The only chapter that doesn't include part of Angela's story is Chapter 2: Technology, because Angela was trafficked in the late 1990s—before the Internet was everywhere and before traffickers could take advantage of the smartphones we carry in our back pockets. Angela's story is still applicable today, though, because everything that happened to her still happens, two decades later.

In this book, I've tried to honor the victims and survivors like Angela; the organizations and volunteers who pick them up, drive them to safety, and help them for months or years as they build new lives; the law enforcement personnel who are trying to stop the illegal sale of humans for sex; the juvenile probation officers whose hearts break they as try, and sometimes fail, to keep young people from being lured into a life of trafficking; the faith-based volunteers who love the victims through everything; the lawyers who help survivors reclaim their lives through criminal and civil lawsuits; the educators who use presentations, lectures, websites and books to get the word out; the mental health professionals who help survivors restore their faith in themselves; and all others who do what they can to save people from a life of injustice, abuse and indignity.

Just as all these do, we can all do something.

This is one of the most important human rights
and social justice issues of our time.

GREG ZARZAUR

| one |

Human Sex Trafficking

'I'm way deep in the game'

Angela's story in her own words:

So, I go to this job interview and the guy opens the door to a really nice place. He lives in this beautiful, wealthy area. He has a nice condo and he invites me in. He asks me my age. I had to be eighteen and over, and I was seventeen at the time, so I lied. I had a fake ID that I used. And so, he looks at it and says, okay.

And he tells me, he just lays it on me: "You are going to give body massages to these very rich men. They come in, they pay this much, and this is how much I give you per client. And sometimes they want to go a little further."

And I'm like, "What do you mean, further?"

He said—I'm just going to use the language we used—"You know, jerk them off and things like that. Never any sex here. Just physically touch their privates and those types of things. It's just hand jobs and stuff."

And I'm thinking, I don't want to do that. But the money was so good. And so, I'm seventeen years old, I'm lured into that money right away. And the guy is very nice. I mean, he never hurt me or anything. Next thing you know, I'm spending all my time doing this. And he's teaching me about penal codes, which is how to not get caught by the police. But now I'm realizing this is not legal, and I'm way deep in the game. Any of these people could be a cop, and I could go to jail for doing this. This is solicitation and prostitution. But I would not allow myself to recognize that at all.

So, I did that for a year.

Nobody knew in my life. I was just making so much money, and they didn't know where I was getting this money from. I lied to my boyfriend and told pretty much everyone I was doing this real estate thing and they were giving me some commissions. They were like, "You're seventeen years old." But I guess they didn't want to see what was right there in their face. How does a seventeen-year-old make this much money and buy all these things and live on her own like this? They didn't want to see.

And I was also really depressed. By now, to keep doing this, I'm on coke because I do feel guilty, I feel terrible sometimes. These are men that are married, from rich men from Wall Street to Hasidic Jews with their huge curls that would come in for a body massage with the full package.

This is a booming business. I mean, every day, the phone is ringing nonstop and they want their body rubs. And they're willing to pay and tip huge. At this point I'm like, I'm not going to let them take advantage of me, I'm just going to start stealing. So, they would come in, they want what they want. And after a while, I'd have repeat clients. And some of these repeat clients are now asking for sex and they're going to pay me a lot. And they don't know I'm this young. Really, to be honest, they don't really care. It's very private, it's secret, so secretive. We were in this back room, hidden. *Nobody knows what's going on there. So, it turned to sexual things because men were asking for it and paying me so much.*

And so, I'm making a lot of money now, like, $2,000 a week. And on top of that, I'm also stealing money from them when they go to the bathroom. They have, sometimes, $3,000 in cash in their back pocket. I'm taking $500, $600 in addition to the tip and the money they paid me. Things are getting really crazy. I'm using more and more drugs to numb myself and deal with it.

After a year doing that, I decided to try to get out of this. So, I saved a nice bunch of money, which got stolen from me by a family member from under my bed. And so, that money was all gone that I worked and saved to get out of this.

Not long after that, I went to this other agency that a friend told me about. But she didn't tell me it was anything like that. She didn't tell me what was happening there. And so, I segued from this body rub place and went to this meeting thinking I'd be doing the same thing.

When I get there, it's in this office where there's a bunch of you-rent little offices to do your business—real estate, insurance, title, escrow, whatever. And then this room, like 206 or something, and you go in and you wonder, what the hell am I going into? And there's these Russian men there. There were about four of them. And then there's this lady picking up the phone, and men asking for certain types of women, like, "I'm looking for a brunette, Hispanic, thin, for full sex."

This is now turning into full escorting. They call it escorting, but you're not escorting anyone anywhere, you're just going and having sex with people at their house. You're being delivered from place to place in a car that they rent. And they're very controlling and strict. They want to know where you're at. That's why they have a cab waiting for you outside, to make sure you get the money. And they're going to get their cut.

So now, I'm just in full prostitution. I'm about to turn eighteen. Once again, I lied, I told them I'm eighteen. They say to me when I come in for this interview, "Drop your clothes." And I'm like, "Huh?" I've never just gotten naked in front of people like that I've never met, and they're all just sitting there staring at me. He said, "Take off your shirt, take off your pants and turn around." I mean, it was just degrading at that point. But I didn't know how to say no. I'm already there, they're looking at me, and I'm just thinking, what am I getting myself into? But I don't know how to get out of it now, because I'm here. And I didn't even know this type of thing existed, to be honest, that's how ignorant I still am.

So, they give me my first call, "We'll start you tonight. You're available?" And still, they're not telling me what I'm starting. But I'm like, "Okay, sure." I really did believe, naively, I would be dressing up and going somewhere with someone, escorting them to an event. I had no idea what this was really going to entail. I find myself once again being naïve. They said, "Somebody wants someone like you, dark hair, dress this way. We have this cab service and he's going to take you there and he'll bring you back."

It was several months of that, that I kept getting driven places. Sometimes it was an all-night thing, three different partners. I felt like I couldn't get out of it. They called me every day, and I had to go. I had to keep it quiet. You're not allowed to talk about it. I did meet other girls who were involved in it. A lot of them were Russian and Yugoslavian and from other cultures who came here. They had no money and got immediately entangled in this like I was. And we weren't really allowed to talk to each other about clients or anything. I'm getting delivered to different houses all the *time. And the funny thing, not every one of them wanted sex. Sometimes they just asked me to sit and talk to them. Or they have, what is it called, a fetish. They want to look at your toes or some weird freaking thing.*

I started seeing a lot of men in hotels. I remember smells, like cologne smells and things. And I didn't want to do it anymore, like, I don't want to have sex with this stranger, this nasty person. It's just some gross people. You could just tell that's why they get prostitutes. They have no other outlet in life. They hide in hotels. Sometimes they would just sit and talk to me. They felt bad for even having a prostitute. They felt guilty. So, some of them didn't do anything, and they still paid me. Those were the lifesaving ones, where I felt so relieved not to do anything.

One night, Angela was arrested and went to jail on solicitation charges, as is explained in Chapter 5. Below is the continuation of her story after she was released from jail.

I was still not telling anybody about this secret life of mine, you know, being controlled with phone calls all day to come do this and do that, pick up here, pick up there and go deliver yourself here and there in this black car. I never told anybody. And I didn't know how to tell these people, "I'm not going. I'm not showing up." I just got really nervous about it. I remember I just shut my phone off so nobody could reach me for a while.

At this point, I decided to go live with my mom for a little bit. [As we'll see in later chapters, Angela's mother was addicted to crack and was selling her own body for drug money.] Leave my boyfriend and try to segue out of that situation without telling anyone, because I was so embarrassed and scared that this has been going on almost two years. It just started with the body rubs and ended in full sexual solicitation every day, almost. Honestly, I still don't tell people that. My husband doesn't even realize to that extent, because that's how shameful it is. It was always in the dark. It could be in the Waldorf Astoria to the cheapest, nastiest hotel. You never knew who the client was going to be.

And they do trap young girls. They do know you're lying because you really do look so young. And then they try to empower you with money. They know you can't get out of it once you make that money because you have no one.

None of these girls were girls of any success or anything. They come because they have nothing and it's the last resort. And they [the traffickers] capitalize on it. To say no is very hard for the girls, too, because they're like, "After all we've done for you, all the money we've paid you, we need you. You need to be here." They try to make it like a real job.

I felt so trapped. I didn't know how I was going to get out because I didn't feel like anybody would take care of me if I did leave that type of lifestyle.

Some people will still shame you, even in the church. Some people just don't know how to handle those things. They say, "Oh, but you had a choice. You didn't have to." They don't understand these people are like incredible mind geniuses. They know exactly what to say to you. They know exactly who to appeal to. They know exactly how to get you to do what they want, and to stay under their thumb for as long as possible. Yes, I went home most nights, but I always knew they were going to be calling and harassing me again. And they do know your address, and you do think they're going to kill you. They had offices that they changed over and over, so they could never be located.

I wasn't allowed to speak about it to anyone because they made clear threats that, "It's illegal and you're going to get in trouble and you'll go to jail and it'll be your fault. They won't know where we are."

Below is Angela's response when I asked if the word "trafficking" was in her vocabulary at that time in her life. I asked if she realized that's what was happening to her.

To me? No, never, never, never, never. Because they made it like it was my choice to take my clothes off, to go to these places. They made me feel like it was my choice. But then the harassment, the control issues. Withholding money, making sure someone was watching me when I was there. Not for my safety, but literally parked outside, waiting for me. And taking me places and not being able to leave the situation once I was in it. It was a very, "you need to finish what you started" kind of thing. It was very scary. But I just felt like I signed up for this, so I'm the bad guy here.

Here, I told Angela that everybody I've interviewed has told me about the psychological hold that traffickers and pimps have over their victims. She interrupted me with:

Let me tell you something, I have a hard time calling them pimps. See the hold there? I just can't. That's like bringing myself lower, to the point that I had pimps in my life—several of them, from the Russian guys to the guy at the massage parlor. I was under their control. And then there's also fear of getting in trouble with the law. They immediately put that fear in you. They're not going to get in trouble, it's you.

I tell people all the time, "You don't know where I've come from." I always say—and they don't even know when I say this that I've already been prostituted—I say that I could have been a prostitute on the street. See, I was not on the street. I was in this whole covert system called all these little names on the back of your newspaper. And once you get sucked into that, it's a long process out. It is a long process out.

* * *

WHAT IS SEX TRAFFICKING?

Was Angela a real sex trafficking victim? The answer is yes.

If you'd asked me that question before I started researching for this book, I might have said no. She chose to take the job at the illicit massage parlor. At the escort business, she answered the phone when the Russian pimps called. And she went home each night—no one was locking her up. At both jobs, she kept part of the money she made.

But, I would have been wrong. Angela was a trafficking victim. For one reason, she was a minor. Also, a third party was benefitting from her commercial sex acts. In the escort business, Angela's traffickers controlled her with intimidation and threats. That's called coercion, which is explained below. This chapter and the following chapters explain more fully what is, and what isn't, sex trafficking.

Sometimes sex trafficking is hidden, but too often it's in plain view and not recognized or acknowledged. In all cases, victims are demoralized while traffickers profit from this form of modern slavery. In all cases, human trafficking is a violation of basic human rights.

Two of the most-discussed forms of human trafficking are labor and sex trafficking. Across the world, almost twenty-five million people are victims of labor and sex trafficking (*Polaris*).[1] Some sources also examine illegal organ harvesting, recruitment of child soldiers, and forced and child marriages as forms of human trafficking.[2]

Labor trafficking occurs when adults or children are forced to work for little or no pay. This is common with immigrants and is often seen in agriculture, domestic jobs, restaurants, cleaning services and carnivals (*Polaris* [Human Trafficking]).

Sex trafficking happens when a person or organization profits from a commercial sex act performed by someone else. A commercial sex act means something of value is exchanged for sexual services.

Human sex trafficking happens to adults and children, to people living in poverty and in wealth, to educated and uneducated people, to every race and culture, to drug addicts and people who have never used drugs. It happens in cities, farming communities, urban areas, rural areas, the suburbs, the mountains, the deserts, the coasts. It happens in schools, churches, homes, sports teams, community centers, on the streets, in shelters. It happens online and in person.

The traffickers themselves are mothers, fathers, stepparents, grandparents, aunts, uncles, cousins, friends, boyfriends, coaches, teachers, pastors, employers, neighbors and sometimes strangers, especially when traffickers use the Internet.

The buyers—mostly men, but not always—are husbands, fathers, doctors, mechanics, factory workers, writers, pastors, teachers, actors, bankers, politicians, executives.

The lists are endless. Human sex trafficking does not discriminate.

One of the biggest misconceptions is that sex traffickers kidnap people and take them across state lines, but it is rare for sex trafficking victims to be abducted by a stranger. Most sources say only three to ten percent of sex trafficking victims are kidnapped.

Another misunderstanding is that human trafficking is the same as human smuggling. The smuggling of humans "refers specifically to violating a nation's laws regarding entry" and is usually done with the individual's consent. With human trafficking, by contrast, "traffickers employ some form of control over their victims" and victims do not consent (Stickle, 10-11). In addition, human smuggling is a crime against the state where the commodity is a service provided (movement of a person), whereas human trafficking is a crime against an individual and the commodity is an individual for sale (Stickle, 27).

Thousands of new human trafficking cases are reported every year worldwide. The 2021 Trafficking in Persons Report, published by the U.S. government, estimated 123,664 new sex and labor trafficking cases across the world in 2020 ("Trafficking in Persons Report 2021"). In the United States, the anti-trafficking organization Polaris reported 16,658 new sex and labor trafficking victims and survivors in 2020 (*Polaris* [2020 U.S. National]). Those figures are based on calls and texts to Polaris's hotline.

However, this is not the full story. Polaris is only one organization. Plus, no one really knows how many people are trafficked because it often goes unreported. "There's no national repository. You've got different groups that have hotlines and take calls, but they're only recording the people that call. ... It really underestimates what the problem is in totality," said Douglas Gilmer, a federal law enforcement agent in Birmingham, Alabama, who works with human trafficking victims.[3]

It's hard to convince some people that sex trafficking even exists, according to Kathy Wilson, Cofounder of the Cullman County (Alabama) Human Trafficking Task Force.[4] "I think that's the most difficult part," said Wilson. The task force sets up a booth at various events every year to raise awareness of human trafficking. "People will literally laugh and just think you're crazy," she said.

I think people laugh because they don't understand that human trafficking happens everywhere, even in rural counties. I learned about people's lack of concern in 2018 when I volunteered to staff the Cullman task force's booth at the county fair. I was nervous at first because I was afraid people would ask questions that I couldn't answer. I hadn't yet started the research for this book. It turned out that my fear was for nothing. I saw people eye the big sex-trafficking poster behind me, then avoid looking at me when they walked by. A few folks did smile and politely take the pamphlets that I offered, but for most of my four-hour shift I stood there alone and watched people crowd around the community college's booth across from me. The college was handing out some great swag.

That night, it sunk in that people simply don't know how wide-spread sex trafficking is, or what it actually means. By 2020, three sex trafficking cases were working their way through the courts in small Cullman County alone.

Wilson pointed out that people are also skeptical about human sex trafficking because of the very term. "I hate that name. I wish the government would change it to human exploitation, because when you hear trafficking, people think of movies," she said. "Being put in a van and hauled off to be sold to the highest bidder somewhere. That's not the way it happens. I want to break that stereotype." Teresa Collier also dislikes the name, for the same reason. "Really, human trafficking is human exploitation. Human trafficking is a crime against a person. It doesn't mean that person is being taken all over the country," said Collier. "You can have a kid that's being trafficked out of their own home and they never even leave their home." Collier is a former Intelligence Analyst for the Alabama Law Enforcement Agency, where her specialty was human trafficking. She's also a Forensic Child Interview Specialist and a trainer for the

Child Trafficking Solutions Project. She has a Master's degree in Homeland Security and Emergency Management.

Another stereotype is that sex trafficking victims are prostitutes. Sex trafficking and prostitution are not the same. With prostitution, an adult chooses to perform a sex act with someone for payment. She or he arranges the transaction and keeps all of the money. Prostitution is illegal in most parts of the United States, but it still does not constitute the crime of human sex trafficking. With prostitution, there typically is no third party involved to arrange the "date" or collect payment. However, in the case of legal prostitution, such as in parts of Nevada, some prostitutes work in legal brothels where a third party does make the appointments and handle the money.

In sex trafficking, however, there is always a third party involved —the trafficker. In sex trafficking, the sex act is not consensual. It is a commercial sex act where the victim is sold for money or traded for drugs, alcohol or anything else of value.

The legal definition of human sex trafficking says that an adult victim is performing a commercial sex act (exchanging sex for something of value) through force, fraud or coercion. The law is different for minors. If a victim is younger than eighteen, a commercial sex act is automatically deemed sex trafficking. Proving force, fraud or coercion is not necessary with minors who have been sold for sex. That's why there's no such thing as a "child prostitute." All minors being sold or traded for sex are trafficking victims.

With adults, all three means—force, fraud and coercion—are commonly used to recruit and retain sex trafficking victims. Here are some examples.

Using force, traffickers might beat or restrain the adult or child victim. Many traffickers also use drugs to force victims' compliance. Angela's traffickers drove her to the "dates" and forced her to complete them even when she said she didn't want to. "Even though I'm already feeling exhausted by this type of living, I can't say no. They have my address, they know where I live, these people are crazy," Angela said.

The second means, fraud, happens all the time. One common ploy is to advertise for modeling jobs, which hooks countless young people. Traffickers talk them into showing up for job interviews, where they spend money on the victims for photo shoots, lodging, food, clothes, makeup and other expenses. Then they tell the victims something like, "We spent all this money on you, now it's time for you to pay up." They arrange dates for the victims, where they are required to have sex. Of course, the victim receives very little or no payment, and is required to go on dates with more and more men. In Angela's case, the ad for the fraudulent massage job tricked her when she was seventeen. "I saw this ad and it looked really clean. 'Give massages, we'll train you, you make this much money,'" Angela said. "So, I just didn't know."

Coercion, the third means, is a psychological tactic. It includes manipulation and "mind games." Amy Wagar, an advocate for Worthy² (Worthy Squared) and a trainer for the Child Trafficking Solutions Project,⁵ met a survivor whose trafficker had threatened to put her infant in a microwave and turn it on. He also threatened to kill the woman's grandmother, who was his neighbor. "What option does she have?" said Wagar. "As a mother, I'd be doing the same thing. Whatever it takes to protect my child. She really didn't have an option." Angela's traffickers also used coercion by making her believe they would kill her if she didn't answer her phone and agree to the dates. "It's the control they have over your mind," Angela said. "More than the physical, it's the mind that they develop the control over."

DEMAND

In the United States, buyers spend $5.7 billion a year to purchase sex, according to Demand Abolition's 2018 research report called "Who Buys Sex? Understanding and Disrupting Illicit Market Demand" (15).

The people who buy commercial sex are the people who create the staggering demand for it. Traffickers are more than happy to supply women and children to meet the seemingly insatiable demand for paid sex.

"Every time we rescued a victim, there was a trafficker ready to drop two more in their place, specifically and solely because of the demand for commercial sex," said Tuscaloosa Police Lieutenant Darren Beams, who founded the West Alabama Human Trafficking Task Force. "It's like any other business. It's what drives the market."

Ignoring demand, which discounts the role of sex buyers, "makes no sense and trivializes the harm done by the buyers," wrote Rachel Lloyd in *Girls Like Us*. She added that the survivors she serves at Girls Educational and Mentoring Services (GEMS) in New York make no distinction between pimps and sex buyers when it comes to the way they're treated. "If asked who's worse, pimps or johns, most would not be able to choose. They've experienced rapes, gang rapes, guns in their faces, beatings, sadistic acts, kidnappings—all at the hands of johns" (111).

John is a nickname for commercial sex buyers.

"*John* is in some way a fitting moniker for men who buy sex. Like *John Doe* and *Dear John*, the name is used as the generic catchall for the anonymous everyman who makes up the millions of men in America who buy sex from children [and from adults]," wrote Lloyd. "Those of us who have been exploited by the sex industry know that johns represent every walk of life, every age, every ethnicity, every socioeconomic class. Judges, mailmen, truck drivers, firemen, janitors, artists, clergy, cops, drug dealers, teachers. Handsome and rich, poor and unattractive, married, single, and widowed. Fathers, husbands, sons, brothers, uncles, neighbors (107)."

Wagar makes the same point: anyone can be a sex buyer. When I interviewed Wagar for this book, she turned her laptop around so I could see the document she was reading from. It was a "john spreadsheet." The information on it came from questions she and other anti-trafficking advocates asked men after they were arrested for buying sex. The spreadsheet tracks the buyers' age bracket, race, marital status, where they live, and their gender. (At that point, no females had been arrested in her area for buying sex.) "We ask if they've ever been robbed or assaulted when paying for sex," said Wagar. "It's a very violent lifestyle."

They also track the men's occupations. "We've had several pastors get arrested," said Wagar, including one who was planning to lead worship the next morning at a church where he had just accepted a job as youth pastor. Wagar said the man didn't get the job after all.

Arrests in Tuscaloosa have also included construction workers, soccer coaches, university employees and university students. "We had a student come in one night—he paid for his sex with a Ziploc bag of rolled coins," Wagar said. In another case, a man was helping his child move into a college dorm one weekend. "The kid went to hang out with some friends, the dad went to meet up and have some sex and got arrested," Wagar added.

The john spreadsheet includes all income levels—wealthy and low-income people from across the state. "It's everybody," Wagar said.

The advocates also ask the men where they saw the sex ad, what made them buy sex that night (porn and sex addiction are common answers), how often they watch porn, how old they were when they first saw porn, and how much they paid for sex ($60 for a "low-end situation and a low-end pimp" up to $120 or more for sex purchased online, according to Wagar).

Wagar works alongside police departments in Birmingham, Tuscaloosa and other cities in Alabama. She and Beams, of the Tuscaloosa Police Department, worked together to create the questionnaire for sex buyers.

Beams argues that the only way to eradicate sex trafficking is to address the demand. One solution, he said, is to punish sex buyers more severely. "Right now, there's just a slap on the wrist for johns," Beams said. "We've got to get judges and prosecutors on board to make the punishment more severe for the johns because if you don't do that angle, a trafficker is going to see that market for what it is. It's a lucrative market, and they're going to see that there's a lot of money in it. It's supply and demand just like anything else. If you drive the demand away, then the supply dries up."

Since Beams doesn't have the power to change state law, he has tried other approaches to stem sex trafficking in his city.

When he was in charge of the Tuscaloosa police division that investigates human trafficking, Beams organized numerous undercover operations to target sex buyers. At the time, the police department had the pictures of commercial sex buyers published in the local newspaper. "I took some flak from the community about that, because everybody said we were train-wrecking families," Beams said. "Listen, if your husband goes to buy commercial sex, your marriage is already train-wrecked. I didn't wreck it. He did."

Beams' goal was to make people think twice before buying sex in Tuscaloosa. "I want them to think, 'I wonder if she's an undercover police officer,'" Beams said.

Even though his approach was controversial, it got results. "Successful prosecution of the sex buyer does work," Beams said.

The recidivism rate is his proof. The national recidivism rate for sex buyers is thirty percent, according to Beams, meaning almost one-third of johns are repeat offenders. But in Tuscaloosa, the recidivism rate was less than one percent. Of 330 johns arrested while Beams was in charge of the vice unit, only two were arrested a second time for buying sex. "That tells me that my program was working," Beams said.

Lisa Thompson agrees that addressing demand is crucial in the fight against human sex trafficking. Thompson, Vice President and Director of the National Center on Sexual Exploitation's Research Institute in Washington, D.C., uses the image of a tree to demonstrate her point. She said some people think risk factors such as lack of education, drug addiction or child abuse are the roots that support and sustain sex trafficking. "But I want to posit that the main supporting structure holding up all of the sex trafficking tree is the issue of demand," said Thompson. "It's the sex buyers who ultimately sustain this whole enterprise."

Thompson asks a good question: "Who are these people?" The people who purchase commercial sex are mostly men. "They come from all ages and socioeconomic levels, occupations, ethnic and racial groups," she said.

In the "Who Buys Sex?" research report mentioned above, Demand Abolition further answers the question of "who are these people?" The organization found that although most sex buyers are men, most men do not purchase commercial sex. Twenty percent of the 8,201 men surveyed had illegally purchased commercial sex at least once, with only six percent of men saying they had paid for sex within the past year (9).

The study found that ten to twelve percent of U.S. men were "actively engaged in sex buying within a 12-month period." Most men had purchased sex two to five times, with twenty-five percent of that group saying they had bought sex more than ten times (9).

The group of men who buy sex more than ten times a year are called high-frequency buyers, meaning they purchase sex at least weekly or monthly. The high-frequency buyers have a huge impact on the U.S. sex trade—they make seventy-five percent of the sex purchases in this country (16).

It's clear from the billions of dollars that sex buyers spend in the U.S. that demand isn't going away anytime soon. Because of this demand, traffickers have no financial incentive to stop selling human beings for sex.

TACTICS OF TRAFFICKERS

Traffickers have plenty of ways to target victims. Polaris identified twenty-five "business models" for human sex and labor trafficking. The data is based on almost 17,000 cases, including phone calls to Polaris's National Human Trafficking Hotline from 2007 to 2016, and text messages to their BeFree Textline from 2013 to 2016.

The two most common sex trafficking business models are the same two that hooked Angela. The most common, by far, is escort services, with 4,651 sex trafficking cases. The second-most prominent model—with 2,949 sex and labor cases—is illicit massage, health and beauty operations. A few other business models also include sex trafficking victims: outdoor solicitation, residential sex trafficking, pornography, personal sexual servitude and remote interactive sexual acts (*Polaris* [Typology]).

These statistics are an excellent snapshot of trafficking business models, although, as the website points out, they do not necessarily represent the true scale of trafficking in the United States because many victims never call or text the hotline.

Countless victims are afraid to reach out for help, and they are right to be afraid. "It's a business for the traffickers, and they run it like a business. They know their stuff. They're cunning and cruel and they know every detail that they can get," said Wilson. She warns people to never personally intervene in a suspected trafficking situation. "Because you're putting yourself in jeopardy," she said. "It is a business. And if you stop their business, you stop their income. They'll kill you for that."

The income is no slight matter. Worldwide, human traffickers make close to $150 billion every year in profits (Stickle, 2).

The twenty-five business models that Polaris identified show us various ways that traffickers make money from victims' commercial sex acts. But how do traffickers lure their victims in the first place? Wagar explains some of the approaches that traffickers use.

One way is the "guerilla" approach. "They're the violent ones," Wagar said. "They're going to use force or threat of force." Wagar saw this one night when her team was doing street outreach at a hotel and saw a pimp beating up a woman. Wagar reached for the door handle to get out of the car and help the woman. A security member on her team grabbed her shoulder and sat her back down. "He said 'You'll make it worse for her, and you'll get beat up too,'" Wagar said. "And he was right."

Another approach is the "business" trafficker, where he gives the victim a cut of the money. "They'll present it more as a business option, and they'll coerce someone into it before they even realize that they've been talked into doing it," said Wagar. "They are psychologists." This is what happened to Angela. When she took the job at the massage parlor, she got a portion of the customers' payment. At seventeen years old, she was overwhelmed by the amount of money she could make. There's no doubt that her trafficker made much more money than she did.

A third approach is the "lover boy" model, which also uses coercion. "He'll say, 'This is a family thing. I love you. You love me. We just need fifty dollars to make ends meet. I hate to do this, but

I've got a friend who said he really likes you and respects you. And if you sleep with him, he'll give us fifty bucks to make the bills we need,'" said Wagar. "Before long, it's twenty more friends and, 'Can you go dance at this club?'"

The lover-boy model often goes hand-in-hand with familial trafficking, where the trafficker victimizes family members or other vulnerable people who are close to him. Familial trafficking is on the rise, according to Polaris. In 2020, recruitment by family members or caregivers was up 47 percent and recruitment by intimate partners was up 21 percent (*Polaris* [2020 U.S. National]).

Familial trafficking is especially common with children. Unfortunately, anti-sex-trafficking experts have countless stories of familial trafficking. "We've had parents who actually would trade their child to the neighbor for a case of beer," said Wilson. Collier told about a woman who was addicted to opiates letting her eighty-seven-year-old boyfriend rape her fifteen-year-old granddaughter in exchange for drugs. "Every once in a while, you'll see those cases that make the news, but the truth is, there are a whole lot of cases that never make the news," said Collier. "I'm seeing an uptick in those types of familial trafficking cases."

In familial trafficking cases and other situations where traffickers use coercion, grooming is a key part of the process. Grooming happens when traffickers take weeks, months or years to carefully build a relationship with the intended victim, working hard to gain her or his trust. Grooming is common in sex trafficking, but is also common when someone plans to exploit a victim for his or her personal sexual gratification, which is not the same as trafficking. When traffickers and other sexual predators are grooming a victim, they can be very patient. Sometimes they pretend they're helping the victim with a problem. Sometimes they pretend to love the victim. "They'll come at you as a wolf in sheep's clothing," said

Wagar. "And they start building a relationship, and it can be a long con. A trafficker is an expert at picking out vulnerability, which is what trafficking is. If you boil it down to the absolute nuts and bolts, it's the exploitation of vulnerability."

A trafficker can go into a crowded area and immediately pick out the most vulnerable person. He looks for someone who has her head and shoulders down, someone with obvious low self-esteem. He might tell her she's beautiful, she has pretty eyes, she caught his attention from across the room, there's something special about her. "They're not going to go after the kid who's loud and who's going to fight," said Wagar. "They want an easy target. They'll say, 'I'd love to hang out with you sometime.' It's a con." Wilson said traffickers will sometimes give lavish gifts and promise to take care of the victim. "And once they build that trust and that rapport, then the victim more than likely goes willingly because they think they're going to a different life than they have," she said.

Wagar knows of a survivor whose trafficker befriended the parents and even paid for tutoring for the child victim. "So, they're conning the parents as well, sometimes," she said. "They don't come in and say, 'I'm going to kidnap you and cause you to have a horrible life.' They sneak in there on the sly and do what they can do to establish trust and rapport. They take control of their lives before they ever have a clue that their life has been taken control of. So, by the time a victim or a survivor gets in front of an advocate or law enforcement, you have to explain to them that something bad and illegal has happened to them."

Another tactic of traffickers is to physically mark their victims, especially when they are exploiting several people. Many traffickers force their victims, whom they consider to be their property, to get tattooed or branded with the trafficker's symbol. It might be the trafficker's initials, street name, a barcode or other symbol. A recent trend is to tattoo victims with invisible ink that can only be seen with a blacklight. "You can get more money for a victim who doesn't have a tattoo branding," said Wagar.

Traffickers are constantly changing their tactics to avoid getting caught. Organizations that work with victims and survivors must continually learn the newest tactics. "There are always new trends," Wagar said. "Trying to keep up and understand what's going on and sharing data and information with others in the fight is really crucial. Things are always changing."

One thing that doesn't change is misconceptions about traffickers. One is that sex traffickers are hiding in an underground network of criminal activity. In fact, they often have regular jobs and active social lives, spending time with people who have no idea that they sell human beings for sex. From her work as a survivor advocate, Wagar has dealt with plenty of traffickers. "There's one pimp that I know, he lives not far from where we're sitting right now. He works out at a nice, popular gym near here," she said. They often easily blend in. "They have jobs, families, friends, and often hold positions of authority within their own community," wrote Amy Joy in *Human Trafficking 101: Stories, Stats, and Solutions*.[6] "The truth is, you don't know who a trafficker or predator is simply by looking at them. It is not indicated by the clothes they wear or anything else. They look just like you and me; every [race], age, gender, culture, and creed" (76).

CULTURE

There is a wide range of awareness about human sex trafficking. Some people have barely heard of it, like me before I heard the speaker from The WellHouse in 2012. While I was working on this book, I would tell friends and family about things I'd learned.

They, too, were usually shocked about how common sex trafficking is, and how easily people get trapped into it. On the other end of the spectrum is people who see or experience sexual exploitation every day.

For the first group, there is a culture of innocence regarding human sex trafficking. "Not in my neighborhood." "Not in my school." "Not in my church." "Not my friends." "Not my child." These are misconceptions. "When people say that human trafficking doesn't occur in their town, they're wrong. It's happening everywhere," said Gilmer.

Angela is in the second group. Long before she was a trafficking victim, she saw sex workers and drugs in her neighborhood every day. At age five, she lived in a run-down hotel where prostitutes and drug dealers solicited out front and at the bakery next door. "People would just rent the hotel out for sex then move on to their next place. But we lived there," she said. "And to my mom, this was nothing. We would just be down there with her. My mom wasn't a prostitute at the time, but I'm sure she was doing questionable things."

Wagar has seen elementary school students who are growing up as Angela did, seeing sexual exploitation as a way of life. "We had fifth-grade students literally pimping out their fifth-grade classmates," Wagar said. "You won't find that everywhere in all schools in all areas. But it's a cultural problem there because the kids are used to seeing people in their community in prostitution if they're trying to make ends meet. It's more accepted in certain cultures."

Because sex work is so familiar to some people, anti-trafficking advocates can't go on the street and offer to help victims get back to a normal life—everybody's "normal" is different. This includes children who accept prostitution as way of life. "They're just so much more exposed to that as a survival option," Wagar said. "But also, to having a pimp, and the actual trafficking being more culturally accepted in certain areas. It's kind of shocking."

Connie Oden, LICSW[7], of Birmingham, Alabama, said the normalization of sexual exploitation is not surprising in some instances. "In many, many cultures, this is just sort of normal," she said, adding that children learn behaviors from the adults surrounding them. When kids grow up surrounded by pimps, prostitutes and sex trafficking, they learn that the illegal sex trade is a viable way to make money.

Trafficking victims also develop their own version of a normal culture, with a unique worldview, rules and lexicon. Oden likened it to a "cult mentality," where their subculture is centered on the trafficker.

Rachel Thomas, M. Ed.[8], of Houston, Texas, has experienced the trafficking subculture. Thomas, a survivor of sex trafficking, is the director of Sowers Education Group and lead author of *Ending the Game: An Intervention Curriculum for Survivors of Sex Trafficking.* "So often, a person's entire identity is wrapped up in 'the life' or in 'the game.' The name that they go by, the style of dress, the future goals for themselves, the daily goals they set for themselves, the rules to live by, the lingo to use. So much of that is consumed and dictated by this subculture. And it really feels like an alternate universe that you're living in," Thomas said. "And so, the way you look at the whole world and yourself is really shifted when you are ushered into this subculture of human trafficking. And whether you're forced in or fall into it through a lack of choice or through drug addiction or the many ways that people get caught up into trafficking, once you're in that lifestyle, you learn to adapt to it. And then after you've adapted, you may even learn to thrive in it or find success in it or feel like your needs are being met in it and find positive aspects of

THE TRUTH ABOUT SEX TRAFFICKING - 33

it. Which just reinforces you into that lifestyle, despite the trauma and the pain and the loss of self."

The trauma and loss of self can help explain why sex trafficking victims and survivors can be standoffish or outright hostile. They frequently do not see themselves as victims and do not want to be treated as such. (There is more about victimology in Chapter 4.) Wagar has seen this plenty of times. "Oftentimes, they don't see you as coming in to rescue them. They're not thankful, they don't want you there. You have to more or less help them become aware that their life is in danger," she said. "They don't realize that a crime has been committed. They don't realize the danger that they're in. It's a very, very violent lifestyle."

As a volunteer at The WellHouse, Penny Billings has seen that it takes time to build a relationship with sex trafficking survivors. "The girl that I mentor is really, really private," Billings said. "Still a year later, she keeps me at arm's length. She's never had anyone to help her and mentor her and guide her. It's hard for her to accept that from somebody." Billings said the survivor that she mentors will barely hug her. Meanwhile, "there are other girls who are just so starved for affection—honest, good, loving affection, that they want to hug all the time."

Anti-trafficking advocates spend time with sex trafficking survivors and therefore get to know them well. But those unfamiliar with victims and survivors have varied and sometimes strong opinions. Some people do not see sex trafficking victims as victims at all. Carolyn Potter, CEO of The WellHouse, said she was surprised to learn how some people react to the women in her program. "I didn't expect that people would view them as they sometimes still do. They view them as prostitutes and this is how they want to make a living and this is a choice that they made," Potter said.

It's true that some of the women in her program have worked as prostitutes without a trafficker "because they didn't know what else they could do to survive," Potter said. "But the majority that we try to help are truly being forced, and there's fraud and there's coercion. There are the elements that the law says you have to have in order to have a trafficking victim. But I have been surprised at that mentality from various parts of our communities that do not see them as someone who needs to be rescued."

As a sex trafficking survivor and an activist who has worked with thousands of trafficked teenagers in New York City, Rachel Lloyd has experienced the community's disdain for victims and has witnessed it in the lives of others. She describes her experiences in her memoir, *Girls Like Us.* "Women in the sex industry, and therefore trafficked and sexually exploited girls, are not believed to be capable of being hurt or raped. In fact, rather than being seen as victims, they're seen as willing participants in their own abuse and are often perceived as having 'asked for it' (126)."

Wagar tells of a woman she met while doing outreach at a strip club. The woman, who had been trafficked as a child, started crying when Wagar and her team walked in. "It just broke me, because I later found out that she was really upset that day because her child was going to a church daycare, and when they found out what she did for a living, they didn't want her and her influence around," said Wagar. The daycare kicked the child out of its program. "If ever there was a time to embrace someone and be the church, that was it. You just totally missed it. This person needs hope. Help. They need to know their value. They need to know that their life matters. And no one is telling them that."

The negative perception can be even more extreme for victims and survivors of color. Dr. Carolyn West, Professor of Clinical Psychology at the University of Washington in Tacoma, Washington, has spent many years researching African American girls and women in the sex and pornography industries. Her research shows that Black girls and women become victims at a higher percentage than other races. "Anybody can certainly be targeted, but Black women are disproportionately more likely to be targeted," said West. She cited a study by the Urban Institute where researchers interviewed pimps. The study found that pimps believed they would spend less time in jail for trafficking Black victims. "White women could make them more money, but that way there would be fewer consequences for trafficking Black girls and women," West added.

Sex buyers also have a more destructive attitude toward Black trafficking victims, according to West's research. She said buyers tend to see Black victims as a "disposable population" that no one cares about. "So, you can be more violent with them. Engage in more degrading terminology with them," West said, adding that the same is true in pornography that depicts Black women. "And so, it makes sense to me why they're going missing at higher rates and murdered at higher rates. Because buyers know that they can target this population and nobody's really going to care and be looking for them if they're missing or if they're injured."

In addition, West found that Black girls and women are dispro-portionately more likely to be arrested for prostitution. "We know that they're victims, and they're survivors. Yet they're being sort of swept up into the legal system. I've seen that happening where I live in the Seattle area, even though we have a very small Black population here," she said.

Other groups are also perceived as having less value, includ-ing indigenous girls and women, and members of the LGBTQ+ community. Indigenous girls and women are "among the popula-tions that are highly vulnerable to human trafficking," according to the Trafficking in Persons Report (17). As for LGBTQ+ victims, Audrey Baedke, Cofounder and Programs Manager of Real Escape from the Sex Trade (REST) in Seattle, Washington, tells of a client who identifies as transgender. The client felt such discrimination from society that she turned to sex work, where she found acceptance. "She said that she feels more accepted in the sex trade than she ever did at any of her mainstream jobs because there she had customers, we will say, that valued her body, that were willing even to pay money for it, in her perspective," said Baedke. "She said they honored who she was and valued who she was."

All trafficking survivors are also vulnerable in the courtroom, where society's perception of them can cause problems, particularly from a jury. Sometimes survivors have a criminal record, often drug or prostitution charges. Many times, however, a victim is doing drugs because a trafficker got her addicted. And it is common for trafficking victims to end up in jail for prostitution because law enforcement officers don't realize they are being trafficked. Having a criminal record tends to make survivors less effective as witnesses in court. "If you put them on the stand, a jury might say, 'Well, she's just a drug addict,' or 'They have a criminal history themselves,'" Collier said.

Potter is quick to clarify the truth about sex trafficking survivors. "These are not just drug addicts. They're not just prostitutes," Potter said. "They are people who—almost one-hundred percent of them—had a very rough start in life. They were abused at the hands of the people who should have taken care of them. And that led to even worse things happening to them. These girls are amazing. They're talented. They're very loving. Anybody who deals with them, they just fall in love with them."

Potter said practically all survivors who have entered The Well-House endured childhood sexual abuse. "And so, if for no other reason, we should be trying to help them," she said. "Because even if we're not seeing them as victims right now, there was a time when they were victimized and this has become their way of life to survive because of their early victimization."

SUBSTANCE ABUSE

Substance abuse is common among sex trafficking victims. When survivors enter recovery programs, their first step is often to detox from drugs.

Sometimes people abuse drugs or alcohol before traffickers ever target them. This gives traffickers an opening to exploit victims by becoming the supplier. Amy Joy's *Sex Trafficking 101* identifies substance abuse as one of several factors that creates a vulnerability in a potential sex trafficking victim (103). Sex traffickers will sometimes hang around methadone clinics,[9] according to Lt. Darren Beams, founder of the West Alabama Human Trafficking Task Force. "They're looking for victims that are already in crisis with a drug problem," he said. "Drugs are a facilitator to trafficking."

In other cases, traffickers will purposely get their victims addicted. Joy writes that traffickers often use drugs in the grooming process to subdue the victim and get her addicted. She then has a strong dependence on him, which allows him to manipulate her and maintain control over her (84).

Substance abuse is common with the survivors who arrive at The WellHouse. Dealing with addiction is a big part of the curriculum. "I did not know how much drug use and substance abuse would be involved in their lives until I started working for The WellHouse. We have had to address all of that, and we're still working on ways to do it," Potter said.

In her volunteer work at The WellHouse, Billings also sees the pattern. "Some girls actually were drugged and that's how it started for them. A trafficker got them addicted and then they were dependent on that drug and the next fix," Billings said. "And in order to get that next fix, they had to do whatever the trafficker told them to do."

Drugs played a big role in Angela's life when she was being trafficked. She started doing cocaine as a way to cope when she started
doing sex work at age seventeen. Even after leaving the life of sex
trafficking, Angela continued to depend on drugs for a while. "I was
still doing coke, trying to numb myself to sleep every night. I tried
to push away everything that had happened," she said. "I felt really
low about myself at this point."

She also used drugs to deal with troubling dreams. "I started
getting scared because these dreams kept coming over and over in
different forms that Jesus comes to the Earth through a bunch of
judgements and people are running and scared. And I'm talking
darkness, real darkness on the Earth. And I'm not one of God's. I'm
not doing his will. Living my life any old way," she said. "And so, I
got kind of tired of these dreams. I tried to ignore them. I'd wake
up, smoke a blunt right away just to numb that kind of thinking.
This is how I dealt with life, just to numb everything."

As an analyst, Collier sees bigger patterns regarding substance
abuse. The United States is in the midst of an opioid crisis, and
more kids are being put into foster care as a result, Collier said. The
Alabama Department of Human Resources reports a thirty-percent
increase in the number of children who have gone into foster care
over the last few years, Collier said, due largely to the opioid crisis.
"It goes hand in hand—if you have a caregiver who has an opioid
addiction and they've got kids that are available to be traded for
drugs, an offender can have sex with the child or time to do whatever they want without supervision," Collier said. "I'm seeing a lot
of increase in the number of those types of cases."

Collier also links sex trafficking, substance abuse and gang
activity. Analysts at the Alabama Law Enforcement Agency have
identified eight gangs operating in Alabama, according to Collier.
In 2017, she partnered with analysts in Georgia, Louisiana, Texas,
Mississippi and Florida to pool resources on gang activity. "What

we found was a huge increase in the number of street gangs that were operating in human trafficking," she said. The analysts informed law enforcement about their findings. "And that's helpful to them," Collier said, "because they may be working a drug case with somebody that's in one of those gangs, and maybe they notice some prostitution that's down the line, too. Only most likely it's not prostitution, most likely it's trafficking. So that just means they can maybe have additional charges and make a trafficking case as well as a drug case."

INDICATORS

Sometimes it's hard to tell when a person is being trafficked. Victims can be good at hiding the clues. At other times, the signs are more obvious. In *Human Trafficking 101,* Joy lists some potential signs that a person is being trafficked. (If you think someone is being trafficked, see Chapter 7 for resources to get help.)

Possible signs of human sex trafficking include:

- Repeated injuries over time
- Repeated symmetrical injuries (patterns made by bite marks, tools, belts, cords, shoes or kitchen utensils)
- Linear or circular burns (often used as a form of torture, punishment, rite of passage or branding to indicate ownership)
- Bruising on the cheek, neck, trunk or buttocks
- Tattoos of names, numbers or barcodes (can indicate ownership)
- Unable to speak for himself or herself (someone else speaks for them)
- Never alone

- Not in control of their money
- Signs of physical or sexual abuse
- Confusion, inability to think straight
- Not knowing what day it is or what city he or she is in
- Lying about their age
- Referring to an unrelated, usually older, male as "daddy" or "boyfriend." Referring to unrelated females as "wifey," "wifey-in-law" or "sister wives"
- Unable to come and go freely
- Working especially long hours
- Receiving little or no pay for work performed
- Working in harsh conditions
- Excessive security measures in the work area, such as fences, security cameras, etc.
- Exhibiting an unusual degree of fear or anxiety
- Coming from, or living in, an abusive home
- Has more than one cell phone
- Is angry, withdrawn or depressed (if symptoms are beyond what is typical for developmental stages)
- Possessing large sums of money, beyond what would be expected for the person's age and type of job
- Lack of parental supervision and support
- Appears hungry or malnourished
- Inappropriately dressed
- Going into high-crime areas (90-96)

These guys are crafty. They're on all the Internet
platforms out there that our kids are on.

DARREN BEAMS

| two |

Technology

'Know what your child is doing'

Angela was trafficked in the late 1990s, when the Internet was nowhere near as commonly used as it is today. That's why this chapter does not include an excerpt of her story. She was coerced into sex trafficking after answering a job ad on the back page of a newspaper. Her traffickers contacted her with a cell phone, but not a smartphone as they had yet to exist. Today, traffickers commonly use social media, online games and various apps to target victims.

Also, in the 1990s, pornography was in demand, but was mostly found in magazines and on VHS tapes. In today's world, the Internet is teeming with countless pornographic sites, as well as websites where consumers can illegally purchase adults and children for sex.

Technology—including the devices that most of us carry daily—is a key component of human sex trafficking.

* * *

DEVICES AND THE INTERNET

Here's the trafficking stereotype: a stranger kidnaps a woman or child, tosses her into a van that disappears around the corner, locks her into a room and forces her to have sex with strangers.

That's great for the movies, but it's not how human sex trafficking typically happens today. Kidnapping is far from the biggest danger that we face when it comes to human sex trafficking. Kidnapped victims are likely to be too much trouble because they'll fight back and refuse to cooperate. It's easier in the long run for traffickers to gain victims' trust through grooming. Grooming online is effective and efficient, as traffickers can groom numerous victims at once.

Today, many sex traffickers use our favorite devices to victimize kids and adults. "Now the man in the van with the candy is in your kids' bedroom on their gaming system, or in the palm of their hand on their phone," said Kathy Wilson, Cofounder of the Cullman County (Alabama) Human Trafficking Task Force.

Many kids do have phones in their hands—or their pockets or backpacks—these days. According to a 2019 Common Sense Media survey, 53 percent of children have a smartphone by age 11, and 69 percent have one by age 12 (Robb).

A fourteen-year-old family member showed me recently how to punch in a code on her smartphone so her number wouldn't show up on the person's phone that she called. She then proceeded to prank call her school friends like we used to do before Caller ID existed. Kids know how to use their devices, often better than adults do. However, technology "street smarts" doesn't translate to wisdom, or even common sense. Children are extremely vulnerable to online predators.

"If you give a kid a smartphone, they're vulnerable. Period," said Amy Wagar, an advocate for Worthy[2] (Worthy Squared) and a trainer for the Child Trafficking Solutions Project. "Kids are being trafficked out of their own bedrooms. Mom can be in the kitchen cooking spaghetti and think her daughter is in her room working on homework. It's a nice neighborhood. And the daughter is being forced to send pictures and videos of herself to people that she doesn't want to."

If people look only for "streetwalkers and prostitutes" being trafficked, they're going to miss it, Wagar said, "because kids who are still going to school and still making good grades are being trafficked in their homes."

In 2020, the number of people being targeted online by traffickers increased by 22 percent, according to Polaris. On Facebook and Instagram, recruiting attempts skyrocketed. "There was a 125 percent increase in reports of recruitment on Facebook over the previous year and a 95 percent increase on Instagram," the organization's website stated (*Polaris* [2020 U.S. National]).

Traffickers are experts at finding vulnerable people, whether in person or online. Children and adults leave not-so-subtle clues of their vulnerability all over their social media platforms. People advertise their loneliness, confusion, angst and discontentment on TikTok, Instagram, Snapchat, Facebook and all the others, not to mention the dating and hookup applications (apps). People post pictures of themselves and their kids in provocative clothing and poses. They forget that everyone seeing the posts does not respect them or love them. They do not realize that most people are trafficked by someone they know, including people they think they're getting to know online. Social media is a gold mine for traffickers and other sexual predators.

More than 750,000 sexual predators are online at any given time throughout the world, according to Reuters (Moloney). Traffickers use the Internet to find victims, and also to market them. About 70 percent of sex trafficking victims are sold on the Internet, according to Joy (67). "Most of it is being done online," confirmed Douglas Gilmer, a federal law enforcement agent in Birmingham, Alabama, who works with human trafficking victims. In the city of Birmingham, Gilmer added, more than thirty websites exist for people to purchase sex. "There is still street prostitution that takes place, but it's not as prevalent as it once was, at least here," he said.

Prostitution migrated from street corners to primarily on the Internet about fifteen years ago, according to Glen Buckley, founder of 731 Rescue in Jackson, Tennessee, and founder of the Scarlet Rope Project.[10] The results are widespread. It is now much easier for traffickers to sell women, men and children for sex. It is also easier for the consumer. "You no longer have to take the risk of driving to the bad part of town and getting robbed, or getting stopped by the police, or coming up with an excuse to leave the house," said Buckley. "You can literally sit in your bedroom or your office or wherever you are on the Internet and set up 'dates' online."

It is difficult to estimate how many people being sold for sex on websites are sex trafficking victims and how many are selling themselves by their own choice. Gilmer said sex trafficking is "extremely under-reported."

Not all online exploitation consists of sex trafficking. Buckley has investigated cases at schools that had not reached the level of trafficking, but had the potential. "It doesn't matter if it's private school or public school," he said. "I've worked cases at some of our private schools where the guys are trading nude pictures of the girls like baseball cards. If it's not trafficking, it's definitely exploitation, which ultimately can lead to trafficking."

The solicitation of nude photos is a favorite scheme of traffickers. They either know the victim already or befriend her online, and gradually talk her into sending a nude photo or video of herself. When she does, the trafficker then blackmails her. Wilson tells of a recent case where an adult male was talking online with a 15-year-old girl in another state. "He was pretending to be some other individual. He had her send him naked photos of herself and then did the extortion," said Wilson. The man threatened to send the pictures to the girl's parents if she didn't send him more nude pictures. Sometimes traffickers threaten to post the photos online so the victim's friends and family will see them.

Lt. Darren Beams, founder of the West Alabama Human Trafficking Force, worked just such a case recently. A freshman college student went to the Tuscaloosa (Alabama) Police Department where Beams works, seeking help. "She had reached a point of psychological despair," said Beams. The teenager, an online gamer, had met a boy in a game's chatroom. Soon, the boy asked her to switch to a texting app. "This young lady thought she was talking to a young guy in Georgia," said Beams. "He asked for some nude photos, and she sent them to him. She didn't know it at the time, but this guy wasn't a college student in Georgia. He was a fifty-something-year-old pedophile."

The man used the nude photos to blackmail the teenager. He threatened to post them on her Facebook account. He also figured out from her social media posts where her parents lived, then texted the girl pictures of her parents' house and threatened to harm them. The photos of the house were cropped images from Google Earth, Beams said, but the girl thought the man had stood on the street and taken the pictures himself.

Against her will, the girl continued to send nude photos to the man. When the photos no longer satisfied him, he made her perform sex acts on herself while he watched on video. Then, he forced the teenager to mutilate herself by using a razor blade to carve his nickname on her inner thighs. "He told her, 'If you don't keep doing what I'm asking you to do, your life is going to be ruined,'" said Beams.[11]

"What frustrates me about communication these days is, you don't have to be on the dark web to be in a deep hole.[12] The Internet is a deep hole. There's no gatekeeper," Beams said. "Eighty percent of trafficking and nude images are transported on regular websites."

Traffickers and other sex predators often take weeks, months or even years to groom someone before exploiting them. Grooming a child to send explicit images is the most common type of Internet crimes against children, according to Teresa Collier, a Forensic Child Interview Specialist, a trainer for the Child Trafficking Solutions Project, and former Intelligence Analyst for the Alabama Law Enforcement Agency. "If an offender then sells those images, it can be charged as trafficking," said Collier. "Or if they give a child something to self-produce the images, that is considered trafficking as well." However, if the offender gets a child to send explicit images without giving that child something of value, and uses the images only for his own sexual gratification, the offender would not be charged with trafficking but charged with another crime such as possessing child pornography, according to Collier.

She said a less common situation, but one that does happen, is when a predator grooms a minor online and talks the child into meeting him in person with the intent of having sex. "This falls under Alabama's 'electronic solicitation of a child' law, and the offender can be charged regardless of whether or not the sex act takes place," said Collier. "If the offender then compels the juvenile to have commercial sex with others, then you are in the sex trafficking realm and sex trafficking laws apply."

Collier tells of a case where a 14-year-old boy from a state in the Northeast tried to meet a friend he was playing an online game with. The boy, who was playing Minecraft with his friend in south Alabama, stole his mother's car and had driven hundreds of miles. He was almost to the friend's house when a state trooper pulled him over. The trooper had just taken Collier's sex-trafficking awareness class for law enforcement officers. He realized something was off with the boy's story, so he called a detective to investigate further. "It turns out this guy who was supposedly his friend, who he thought was his own age, was actually an older man that was a sex offender," said Collier.

Most sexual predators that groom children through online games tend to be pedophiles rather than sex traffickers, according to Buckley. "If I'm a pedophile and I like eight-year-old boys, where's the best place to go on the hunt? It's Call of Duty, right? So really, that's more where we see the exploitation," said Buckley. "They convince them to send a photo or video. We don't see a ton of the traditional human trafficking there. Where we see trafficking would be more like Facebook and things like that."

Facebook and other apps—15,000 new apps are created each week—have become "one of the primary mediums for trafficking," Joy wrote. She added that more than 83 percent of teenagers in the United States have a Facebook account, with an average of 425 Facebook friends each (69). Some people accept social media friend requests from people they don't know, which is dangerous. "Most people are not aware that one in every fifty profiles on Facebook is fake," Joy wrote (69).

Beams recently learned how Facebook is used to facilitate sexual encounters. Investigators in his department had arrested a man in an undercover "john sting" operation, and the man agreed to show Beams how it worked. "There are some sub-levels of Facebook that you don't know anything about," the man told Beams. He then went to one of the sub-levels and typed, "I'm traveling to Huntsville tomorrow. I'm looking for a blond."

Beams watched in surprise when responses immediately popped up. "So-and-so works at the Hotel So-and-so in Huntsville. She's blond. She's going to ask you a bunch of questions, but she's not the police," Beams read. The man then typed, "I'm headed to Mobile tomorrow, I'm looking for a brunette, 18-20 years old." Again, immediate responses told the man the name of a hotel and the name of a woman.

Wagar knows of cases where traffickers used Facebook and other apps to set up twerking contests on social media platforms. Young girls would post videos of themselves doing the provocative dance. The traffickers then have the videos of the girls, and—depending on their privacy settings—all of the personal information that they post on their accounts, possibly including the name of their school, their address, where they work, and their family members' names. The traffickers also could have access to all of the victim's young friends' accounts. Many apps pinpoint users' locations, so the victims are easy to find.

Buckley knows a young woman who was groomed online and then trafficked. A thirty-eight-year-old man used the Internet to groom Alicia Kozakiewicz when she was thirteen years old. In 2002, when Kozakiewicz went outside her house in Pennsylvania to meet the man that had befriended her online, he abducted her and took her to his house in Virginia. There, he chained her in the basement and sexually assaulted her numerous times. "In this form of trafficking, he used a webcam and guys would pay him to watch him do these things to this thirteen-year-old girl," said Buckley. The trafficker let his customers know that he was going to kill the girl. One of the men "grew a conscience," said Buckley, and called the FBI, which investigated and removed Kozakiewicz from the man's house.

Kozakiewicz's story does not end there. After receiving therapy, she started the Alicia Project at age fourteen, where she shares her story and serves as a motivational speaker to groups across the U.S.

and in Canada and Australia (*Alicia Project* [about]). Kozakiewicz is also working to get Alicia's Law—named for her—passed in all fifty states. The law provides a "steady stream of state-specific funding to the Internet Crimes Against Children (ICAC) task forces," according to the Alicia's Law website (*Alicia Kozak*). In addition, Kozakiewicz is an expert on Internet safety. Some of her safety tips are in the following section.

INTERNET SAFETY

As we know, smartphones, tablets, computers and the Internet can be used for harmful purposes. However, users should not be ruled by fear when it comes to using devices and the Internet. By implementing a few safety procedures, users can confidently attend to their work, communication, entertainment, health and other needs online.

Many online safety considerations are common-sense, such as don't put your address or phone number in a social-media feed. Joy's advice is: "Never post anything online that you would not want posted on a freeway billboard" (74). Children, on the other hand, need more help staying safe online because they do not necessarily understand the dangers of sexual predators. "Don't just give your kid a cell phone and pat them on the back and say, 'Have at it,'" said Wilson. "Take some responsibility as a parent and know what your kid is looking at. The gaming systems make connections online to everywhere. Be involved. Know what your child is doing."

Many children—and traffickers—are proficient with devices and apps. The anti-sex-trafficking organization Shared Hope International (SHI), describes several categories of apps that predators commonly use to groom and traffic minors. This is not an exhaustive list but includes some common examples. In a fact sheet called

"Apps," SHI explains five types of apps: microblogging, photo- and video-sharing, WiFi-based messaging, dating, and vault.

Microblogging apps such as Facebook, Twitter, Tumblr and DeviantArt allow users to post short and frequent "status updates," according to SHI. Common features include "posting photos and videos, instant messaging, group messaging, and building an individual profile," and some users even build a "miniature empire online." Many of these apps are known to host pornography.

Traffickers also use photo- and video-sharing apps, which "tend to center around the activity of snapping, editing, and posting photos and videos, which can be seen (and sometimes 'liked') by users' friends or by the public (depending on their privacy settings)," according to SHI. These apps include Instagram, Facebook, Snapchat and TikTok. The danger of these apps is that online predators can harvest a tremendous amount of information about kids and teens. "For instance, a trafficker can learn where a teen likes to hang out, who their friends are, what their interests are, where they live, and more—all by viewing their pictures," according to SHI. "Unfortunately, kids and teens can also become vulnerable to traffickers by over-sharing about their personal struggles or issues, especially if they use hashtags to express themselves." In some of these apps, the messages disappear after a certain amount of time. However, predators can screenshot the photo or message, then sell the image online or use it to blackmail a victim.

The next category is WiFi-based messaging apps, including Kik, WhatsApp, Facebook Messenger, WeChat, Viber and GroupMe. "These apps allow their users to 'text' one another using WiFi instead of cellular data, enabling users to message any other user, regardless of geographical location, without additional fees and, sometimes, without the need to even exchange phone numbers," according to SHI. The downside to these apps, regarding safety, is the anonymity of users. "Traffickers tend to gravitate toward communicating with their victims through WiFi-based messaging apps (rather than through traditional texting) due to these apps' anonymous nature, making it harder for law enforcement to track them," SHI stated.

Dating apps allow strangers to look at people's profiles, which include photos and information such as education, occupation and general location. Well-known dating apps include Tinder and Grindr. Some lesser-known apps are Yubo, Bumble, Hinge, Tagged, Plenty of Fish (POF), Coffee Meets Bagel, Badoo, SKOUT and MeetMe. Dating apps usually have age requirements, but it is easy to lie by simply entering the wrong age or date of birth. "Along with shaping modern dating culture as one where it is normal to 'hook up' (or have sexual relations with a stranger), these dating apps are also a place where traffickers can find youth in search of love and/or physical affection," SHI stated.

The final category is vault apps, which create a "secret vault" for photos, contacts, passwords, Internet browsing and more. These apps appear as one thing but are really something else. For example, many of them appear, and actually function, as a calculator until the user enters a code that opens the "vault" for access to secret information, according to SHI. Examples of vault apps are Fake Calculator, Calculator+, Secret Photo Vault and Private Photo Vault. According to SHI, these apps are not usually used directly by traffickers, but still "frequently appear in trafficking cases." Traffickers will sometimes encourage victims to download these apps to hide explicit images or messages that the trafficker sends them, according to SHI. If a parent checks a child's phone, the app appears harmless until the code is entered and the vault opens to reveal hidden content.

Most of these apps are not necessarily dangerous if used properly. "Just because your children use these apps does not mean they are being groomed by a trafficker," according to SHI. Plenty of resources are available for parents to learn about apps that their children want to download, or have already downloaded. Shared Hope International's website is www.sharedhope.org/internetsafety. Another good resource is the Common Sense Media website at www.commonsensemedia.org.

Parents can also use apps to monitor certain activities on their kids' smart phones. Some of the highest-rated apps that allow parental controls are Bark, Circle, Net Nanny and Qustodio. Many others are also available.

Used wisely and safely, the Internet and Internet-capable devices are wonderful tools for creativity, productivity and fun. Kozakiewicz gives specific advice about Internet safety on the Alicia Project website:

- Teach kids and teens to never share personal information like name, address or school unless it is with a person they already know and trust in real life. Traffickers can use the information to groom kids and to find them.
- Strengthen privacy settings on all social networking sites. Make sure the settings do not change after updates. Many social networking sites publish posts as "public" by default.
- Disable geotagging on all mobile devices. Geotagging can pinpoint and disclose a child's location. It can usually be turned off in Settings, or contact the device manufacturer or service provider.
- Discuss the dangers of "checking in." Some apps allow users to share their exact current location on social media sites.
- Remind kids and teens to choose an online handle, screen name or user name carefully. An online predator can make inferences based on how someone represents himself or herself online, which can prompt the predator to make contact.

- Monitor a child and teen's activity on all devices with online connectivity, including phones, desktop computers, laptops, tablet computers and all handheld and video game devices. Kozakiewicz writes, "Please, do not feel that you are 'spying' on your child or teen. You are the parent. This is your responsibility."
- Know the passwords on all of your child's devices and check them regularly.
- If parents or guardians suspect a child or teen is being cyber-bullied, get the facts and contact law enforcement if necessary. Conversely, teach kids and teens there are negative consequences if they cyber-bully someone else.
- Teach kids and teens the dangers of "sexting," which is sharing explicit texts or photos between devices. Sending or receiving nude photos of minors is child pornography. There could be emotional and legal consequences for the children or teens and the parents.
- Educate yourself on the mobile apps your child or teen is using. Ask for a demonstration and an explanation.
- Maintain open, loving and respectful lines of communication with children and teens while setting enforceable rules. Assure children and teens that they can come to you for help with uncomfortable or potentially dangerous situations (*Alicia Project* [Internet]).

In addition, Joy, in *Human Trafficking 101,* lists some warning signs of possible online traffickers or sexual predators. She said to be suspicious if approached by someone online with any of the following characteristics:

- Having no social media friends in common with you

- Having a very common first and last name
- Profile picture is grainy. Low quality suggests it was down-loaded from someone else's profile or website
- Listing the same interests, hobbies or career as you (suggests they read your profile and are trying to connect with you)
- Their profile was just created and they have no other friends (70-71)

PORNOGRAPHY

Pornography and human sex trafficking are closely linked. The ease of accessing the Internet creates a staggering demand for pornography. As pornography consumers create this thriving market, they unwittingly contribute to sex trafficking. To meet the demand, porn creators sometimes use force, fraud or coercion to make the sex videos that consumers want. Using force, fraud or coercion to compel sex acts is sex trafficking.

"Pornography is the number one demand contributor to sex trafficking," said Wagar, who has accompanied law enforcement on undercover operations and talked to buyers after they were arrested. She said practically all of the buyers were pornography consumers. Most people who purchase sex are addicted to pornography, added Gilmer, based on conversations he's had with sex buyers his agency arrested.

"We want to focus in on this Internet space where women and children are trafficked. We believe it's really propping up the industry and they've been given a free pass for too long," said Dani Pinter, Esq., senior legal counsel for the National Center on Sexual Exploitation (NCOSE) Law Center in Washington, D.C., which targets pornography websites for civil litigation. "We know that many trafficking victims are trafficked into the pornography industry, or their abuse is recorded and then uploaded onto these pornography websites, which knowingly profit off of this material. They do nothing to verify age or consent. And they know that many of the women and children depicted in the videos that they profit from are not there willingly, or are children."

Not all pornography is made with people who are trafficked. Many adults make the films willingly. The problem is, it's usually impossible for a consumer to know whether a video is made with trafficking victims or with willing adults. Some pornography depicts rape and other violence, and viewers can't tell if it is an act or real. There is "no viable way to guarantee that any given pornographic content is consensually or ethically made," according to Fight The New Drug, a non-religious organization that uses science to study the effects of pornography. "'Consent' is a slippery word in the world of porn. [...] When it comes to consent, a 'yes' is valid only if 'no' is a legitimate option" ("How Porn Can Fuel Sex Trafficking").

The article also states that people who turn to making pornography for money are often vulnerable due to a substance addiction or financial hardship, and that "agents and producers often exploit these vulnerabilities in order to coerce performers into producing more—and more hardcore—content." Coercion can include threatening to blacklist people if they don't cooperate, not explaining until the last minute what is expected of them, threatening to withhold pay, and other tactics ("How Porn Can Fuel Sex Trafficking").

Not only is pornography more abusive and more prevalent than ever, but it is more accessible. Viewing pornography is also less risky for kids today, according to Buckley. He said that when he was a teenager, his family had one computer, which was placed in a common area of the house. When he used the computer, he knew his parents were likely to walk by any minute. They would also be the ones to use the computer next and see what he had been doing.

"So, there was a ton of risk in trying to see porn online back then," he said. "You fast-forward to today: there are multiple Internet-capable devices in a house. Most children have multiple devices. It's not uncommon for a child to have an iPhone, and iPad and a MacBook. All these devices that have twenty-four-hour access." Kids not only have the means to spend time online, but they often have the opportunity to do so without being monitored.

Thanks to smartphones and tablets, children are now exposed to pornography at much younger ages. Most people see pornography by the time they are thirteen years old, according to Fight The New Drug ("Why Today's Internet Porn...") Some estimates are even lower. "The average age that someone first looks at pornography is now under ten," said Wagar. "Moving into the state of pornography addiction happens pretty quickly. Within a year or two, those kids may be addicted to it."

The effects of long-term pornography viewing are so harmful that sixteen states have declared pornography a public health crisis, starting with Utah in 2016 ("These 16 States..."). Wagar said this is "in large part because of all the negative associations that pornography has with higher violence rates and crime rates and also, the devaluation of life." Wagar said another reason is because of pornography-induced erectile dysfunction (PIED), which happens when men can no longer function sexually with a "live, warm body" because his sex partner does not match up with what he's been viewing in porn videos. "There are males between the ages of eighteen to twenty-five that are being prescribed erectile-dysfunction medication at an alarming rate because they've been using pornography since they were a kid and all through high school," Wagar said. "Pornography is like a drug."

Not everyone who watches pornography becomes addicted to it. But whether a person is addicted or not, long-term pornography use can lead to changes in the brain that make it difficult to stop watching porn ("Why Porn Can Be Difficult To Quit"). "There's that natural progression to where consumers of pornography have to keep changing the content that they're interested in. There are all these biochemical reactions going on in the brain while you're watching pornography," said Buckley. "And eventually, it's like the drug user. The first time you use methamphetamine, it'll never feel like that again. Each time, you have to take more, and take more often, because you never get that first chemical reaction. And pornography is the same way. So, to get that 'first time I ever saw it' high again, you've got to go experience something new."

Long-term exposure to pornography can lead to loneliness, stress, shame, lack of intimacy, poor self-image, altering how the user views other people, and difficulties with relationships (*Fight The New Drug*). Buckley said relationships can be damaged when "normal sexual relationships no longer do it for you." The lack of intimacy from a damaged relationship can lead to someone seeking sexual fulfillment by purchasing sex. "So now, not only is it a biochemical thing going on in the brain, but also you go elsewhere to seek sexual contact because you're not getting that at home anymore because of the relationship dynamic," said Buckley.

Gilmer confirms that some people who purchase sex are pornography consumers who are searching for something they're not getting at home. "Maybe they're looking for something they've seen in a video or a magazine and their spouse or significant other won't do that for them," he said. "It begins with pornography, and over time the pornography doesn't stimulate them so they have to move on to something else, such as actually paying for sex."

Even if pornography consumers do not get addicted, long-term porn viewers tend to watch increasingly extreme content over time. In his work investigating sex crimes, Buckley has forensically examined countless computers and smartphones and has seen all types of pornography on them. He can tell how long a person has been consuming pornography by the stage of porn he finds on their device or computer.

At first, pornography users tend to watch "soft" porn, said Buckley, which shows nude bodies and "something you might see on HBO."

It then progresses to more hardcore porn, where viewers see actual sex acts performed. "Everything is depicted. There's no more imagination or no guesswork at what's going on under the covers," Buckley said.

When hard-core porn no longer sexually arouses viewers, many turn to a fetish, according to Buckley. He said fetishes can be anything: certain ethnic groups, group sex, interracial sex, urinating on each other, or other acts. "Some fetishes are more deviant than others," Buckley said. "Ultimately, even the fetishes no longer satisfy the craving."

The next step is implementing violence into pornography. "It might be a 'pretend' rape scenario or an actual rape scenario," Buckley said. "The violence adds that extra element. They're chasing that high they got way back when they first got exposed to pornography."

When violence in porn no longer sexually arouses the consumer, he or she finds more extreme content. "From the violence, you usually go into bestiality," said Buckley. He added that bestiality, or having sex with animals, is one of the last steps in watching porn because it is taboo, which adds to the excitement. But even at this level, the consumer eventually becomes desensitized and unable to be aroused sexually.

The final and most extreme step, according to Buckley, is pornography depicting sex with children. "The really worst of the worst are the guys who follow the scale all the way up to child pornography. Then it gets really dangerous, because now they're attracted to children. Only children sexually arouse them," Buckley said. "And sooner or later, the videos and the pictures aren't enough anymore. Then they have to offend on a real child. And that, of course, fuels the trafficking of children."

Buckley said the escalation he described is a general model that does not happen in exactly the same way for every person. "Individuals are different," he said. "You may have an individual who goes through the softcore phase, the hardcore phase, and then straight into prostitution. Or you may have someone that goes up to the fetish phase and then goes into prostitution. So, at any given time on this scale, someone could move toward prostitution."

And, as Wagar points out, up to eighty percent of women in prostitution are actually sex trafficking victims.

Some porn consumers end up on a destructive path, but having a pornography addiction does not make him or her a bad person. Wagar points out that sex buyers and those who are addicted to pornography need compassion. "What led them to that point? What have they gone through?" said Wagar. "They need help. They need hope. They need to know that there is a lifestyle outside of sex purchasing. They need a gentle understanding of what their purchases are actually doing. What hell on earth is that purchase causing someone? A lot of them don't know it."

For information on getting help with a pornography addiction, or to learn more about the link between pornography and sex trafficking, visit Fight The New Drug at www.fightthenewdrug.com.

We as a country have lost our moral compass
when we think it's okay to buy and sell children.

KATHY WILSON

| three |

Children

'You can receive payment for this stuff'

Angela's story in her own words:

My sister and I were four and five when our mom and dad split up.
We were living in this shady, disgusting hotel. That was one of the places
I guess we could afford. We were in this dingy room all the way on the
top floor. And my mom, having this freedom with no husband and just us
two, she started to go clubbing and partying, and she would leave us alone
in this hotel all night. She would say she was coming back, but never come
back until the next morning. She would lock the door and we would be in
this hotel room, trying to make food, trying to take care of ourselves. We
were just so young and ignorant. It was terrible. And she would always
come back and we would always forgive her because we were so little.

Then one day, she told us she wanted to introduce us to a guy she met,
and he was really interested in meeting us. When we met him, he was very

nice. *He took us to McDonald's. At this point we didn't have any real men in our lives. So, we're just happy to be eating, going somewhere with my mom other than her leaving us. And then she started to really get serious with him. And over time, I noticed she started changing.*

I found out later she was on crack. She and her boyfriend now are together all the time. He's living with us part-time. It just started getting terrible. He started pistol whipping her, beating her. She has no way out at this point. She's addicted to crack. He's a crack supplier. It's just the perfect relationship for them. And we're just little kids. I was seeing her friends get cracked up and threaten to jump out the window and kill themselves. And I was just always a bystander, taking this all in at four and five years old.

So, my mom starts leaving him with us, going places and not returning. And he starts turning his eyes on us for sexual pleasure. And my mom's not there, no one's there to watch us, so why not? In the end, he was just a total disgusting molester. And he did this to plenty of kids because he showed me pictures and told me what he did to other kids, and what he would do to my mother if I ever told. He would take a gun out and he would put it there, and he would say he will shoot my mother if I ever told. And so, I listened. I learned very early to just comply. Don't fight. Because every time my sister would fight, she got hit. He picked on her and was mean to her, and he was very nice to me. So, I was like, oh, I do these things, I get my way. This is my young mind working at that time to deal with it. Plus, sometimes he would give us a dollar to go downstairs and get Icees, so I learned really early you can receive payment for this stuff.

That actually came to me today. I was thinking about my story and wondered, where did later in life I learn ... oh, its money exchanged for this. This is where I learned it right away at four or five years old from this guy.

So, my sister is going through the same thing, and we're both just pretty quiet about it. Around five and a half, after it was going on a year, not only were we being molested by this guy, but there were other people in the building that—you know, we're just two kids with no authority over us. We're going into people's homes, getting touched by all kinds of people. It's like everybody was touching everybody and everything was very sexual, and it was just a really evil spirit there.

Anyway, we were constantly kept out of school because we would get lice over and over and over again, and it was coming from the hotel, which was just disgusting. So, they eventually just said, "They can't come back to school until this is dealt with."

At age six, Angela told her mother about the sexual abuse by the mother's boyfriend. At that time, she and her sister almost ended up in foster care, but instead moved in with their aunt and uncle. More of that part of the story is told in Chapter 6.

From five to twelve, I was with my aunt. And things were good. We were in school. Of course, I have all kinds of issues. I thought I could touch anybody, and I was just so unhealthy. I would be rubbing myself in class. I didn't understand these were inappropriate behaviors.

So, my aunt took care of us, took us to church, just loved on us, gave us security at home. I just flourished in that. I really loved it. And my sister just didn't really love it. She always wanted to get out and be back with my mom, sneaking calls or whatever. And I was like, I'm safe, I'm home, I don't have to deal with this crap anymore.

So, at twelve, my dad, who I never see, says, "I want my kids back. I'm doing well, I'm in Puerto Rico, I have a wife and I have three other kids, and I want them." The courts believe him and take whatever paperwork he has. My aunt was just about to initiate adoption. So, we moved to Puerto Rico. I had visited once in a while, but I didn't know Spanish, and I really didn't know anything about Puerto Rico, except that my grandma, who I was very close to, lived there. So, it was really nice to have her come visit.

Soon after, my dad went back on crack. Every day, we'd wake up missing some personal expensive, nice things that we had. We didn't know where they were, and he'd go sell them, get money, do crack. One day you see him walking out with a TV on his back. It's going to be sold, and no more TV for us. And we lived in one of the worst neighborhoods you could ever imagine. There were gun wars. They take you out of school to tell you two houses are going to have war with each other, so they want all kids to stay inside these little brick cement homes we lived in. And we just listened. It was traumatizing, because you would hear the gunshots, you would see the war outside and you would just lock yourself in the hallway and pray. And I remember, that was one of the first times I actually said—I always cry when I tell this part—"I just don't know if God exists anymore. He just abandoned us. And if he's real, why does he allow this to happen, for people to treat kids like this?"

And I was just really angry. I started to allow myself to feel the anger. I stopped wanting to be obedient or listen. I got sick of adults because none of them, I felt, were really protecting us. They were always about themselves. And at any point, I started realizing, we could get shot or a bullet could come through the window. My dad was not very protective because he was out doing drugs most of the time.

So, I started to hang out with the wrong crowd, started drinking, smoking cigarettes whenever I could. Even though I didn't like cigarettes or alcohol, I just did it because everyone was doing it. Anything to kind of numb me at this point. I got really boy crazy. I was always thinking about who was going to love me, what boy was going to like me. That was thirteen, fourteen. I was still pretty much a virgin, like I hadn't ever had sex with a guy. My aunt raised us very modest—don't dress a certain way, don't curse, don't paint your nails.

Then my dad got into a program, and they told us at about fourteen-and-a-half that we were going to be moving back to the states. So, we now lived in a trailer park, so a lot of us in this long double-wide trailer. My dad was still doing drugs, so I ran away. Mind you, I grew up in a middle-class home with my aunt, so this was all extremely impoverished to me. I just felt so abandoned, even by my aunt. Why doesn't she send us clothes, why doesn't anybody help?

I started becoming a real fighter. I fought everybody in school. I'm the tough one, nobody messed with me, and that's how I got suspended, expelled all the time because I wanted to be known as, "Don't mess with me." And that just got me nowhere. So, I ran away. I was constantly rebellious. My dad started calling the cops on me to look for me.

My aunt found out that we were doing really bad. Not us, but my dad. He wasn't able to take care of us. So, my mom, who I hadn't seen since pretty much once-in-a-blue-moon in rehabs growing up, shows up one day at our door with her new husband. And she's pregnant. She's with my aunt and my uncle. They just show up in a van and we were like, "Who are these people?" And then I saw them, and it was shocking because I hadn't been prepared to see my mom. What do I say to her?

I was turning fifteen, and she tells me she's there to pick us up and take us back, that we would be living with her. And I wasn't really happy about that. I would prefer to live with my aunt. But by this time my aunt had too many rules, and I was already very, "I do what I want, when I want, and I'm not listening to any of you." So, my mom took us.

Shortly after living with her, I found out she had HIV, and that she had had a really hard life out there prostituting and doing drugs, doing crack like my dad. She was just in really bad domestic relationships, still getting beat and abused. I was thinking she was going to die. She's still alive today and strong, a beautiful Christian lady, but back then she was just really rough and out of it.

So, then I hit fifteen, and I don't like being broke. I don't like my mom having to pay for everything. She was also really kind of stingy sometimes. She'd lock the fridge because she kind of hordes because she grew up in poverty, too. So, I started to just do things my own way.

* * *

EXPLOITATION OF CHILDREN

We can see Angela's trajectory from severe neglect and sexual abuse at a young age, to anger and distrust as an older child. She needed someone to love her. All these factors made her a perfect target when, at seventeen, sex traffickers entered her life.

A disturbing and heartbreaking fact is that traffickers stand to make a tremendous amount of money from sexually exploiting children. "Fifteen to twenty years ago, most predators from the United States would have to travel outside of the country to do the kinds of sex acts to children they can easily do now in the community where they live," according to Amy Joy's book, *Human Trafficking 101*. "Having sex with children, here in the U.S., is as easy as ordering a pizza" (33).

The United States has become a prime location for sexual predators seeking kids. Droves of international "customers" now travel to the U.S. solely to "have sex with American children," according to Joy (33). "There's an emphasis put on youth and youngness," said Lisa L. Thompson, Vice President and Director of Research and Education at the National Center on Sexual Exploitation in Washington, D.C. "There's a higher profit margin for younger people. So that creates an incentive for the exploitation of minors."

Child sexual abuse is also more common today on mainstream pornography websites, according to Dani Pinter, Esq., Senior Legal Counsel at the National Center on Sexual Exploitation Law Center. Pornography is one of the biggest propagators of child sexual abuse. "Pornographic materials continue to be more and more violent, depict more scenarios of incest, and involve younger and younger children," Joy wrote. "The rate of demand for the rape and torture of children has led to an increased rate in the production and distribution of child pornography. It has also led to an increased rate in those seeking sex from children beyond the computer screen" (37).

Children are usually trafficked in one of two ways.

The first is familial trafficking, which means the trafficker is a child's family member or someone close to the child. "The number one way to traffic someone is to already be in their life," said Amy Wagar, an advocate for Worthy[2] (Worthy Squared) and a trainer for the Child Trafficking Solutions Project. "We're talking a parent, a coach, a pastor, a teacher, a sibling, an aunt, an uncle, mom's boyfriend, dad's girlfriend. Familial trafficking is very common for kids." The opioid epidemic has resulted in even more adults trading their kids or grandkids for drugs, but adults sell children for cash and other items, as well.

The second most common way to target children is through social media and the Internet. Every day, kids fall prey to sex traffickers through their smartphones, tablets and computers. "The most dangerous thing you can give a kid is a smartphone," Wagar said. Traffickers build "friendships" with children through social media or online games. They gradually gain trust, often by pretending to be the same age and to have the same interests as the victim. (More about the link between technology and sex trafficking is in Chapter 2.)

These are the most common ways that kids are trafficked, but they're not the only methods. Traffickers also target people in public places such as sporting events, parks or malls. Dr. Carolyn West, Professor of Clinical Psychology at the University of Washington in Tacoma, Washington, said she has seen children being targeted at their schools in places like St. Louis, Seattle and Tacoma. "I was just always struck by the numbers of pimps who were hanging around outside of schools and openly engaging in trafficking and luring young women," she said.

Predators and traffickers often prepare children for sexual exploitation by grooming them. Sometimes grooming takes place over the child's lifetime because the child knows the predator. After being groomed, victims often trust and even love the person who is exploiting them. It is not uncommon for a victim to lie for and protect her trafficker.

Joy breaks the grooming process into six steps.

The first is to target the victim. "Traffickers and sexual predators know exactly what kinds of human behaviors indicate vulnerabilities," Joy wrote. "These vulnerabilities may be indicated by a child or adult through an online platform or in person." (81).

The second step is to gain the victim's trust. "Traffickers will often spend weeks, even months, grooming and manipulating their way into someone's psyche because trafficking humans is where the money is. Human beings can be sold over and over again, so the amount of time invested is seen as a necessary business tool," Joy wrote (81).

Next, traffickers will fill a need. Many victims are homeless or have "obvious physical needs," Joy wrote. Other victims are looking for attention or affection. Some will be pulled in with expensive gifts. "Whatever the need is, the traffickers or predators are watching and waiting for any opportunity to take advantage," according to Joy (82).

A trafficker or predator will then isolate the victim. One way is by telling the victim things like "nobody will ever love you the way I do" or "they just don't understand our kind of connection." This can eventually lead to "a breakdown in family and friend relationships, leaving only the trafficker as a source of support," Joy wrote. If pretending to love the victim doesn't work, the trafficker will sometimes use threats. "Traffickers may tell victims they will harm loved ones if they do not separate from their support." (83).

In the next step, a trafficker or predator will begin to sexualize interactions. It usually starts mildly, perhaps with the trafficker sitting very close to the intended victim. The next time, he might put an arm around the child. The interaction eventually "progresses into full sexual molestation or rape," Joy wrote. (83-84). In an online relationship, the trafficker might persuade kids to send nude pictures of themselves. Sometimes, the trafficker will show pornography to children. This desensitizes them to seeing and, eventually, performing sex acts (84).

The last step is to maintain control. Sometimes the victim is compliant because the trafficker or predator has gained the person's trust and love. If the victim is not compliant, the trafficker might use "threats or acts of violence, rape, blackmail and psychological violence," Joy wrote (84). Traffickers will also threaten family members.

Anyone can potentially become a victim of sex trafficking. One myth is that only girls and women are sex trafficked, but traffickers also victimize boys and men. "The trend in boys being sexually trafficked is steadily increasing, and the point of entry age is younger than girls," according to Joy. She added that boys make up 44 percent of those trafficked under the age of eighteen (36).

Children who have been in trouble are an easy target for traffickers, according to Glen Buckley, founder of 731 Rescue and the Scarlet Rope Project. He used a made-up example of a twelve-year-old girl from a single-parent home who has been in trouble at school. She has a low self-esteem and, thus, is easy to manipulate. Buckley put himself into the mind of a trafficker. "If she were to go tell on me, nobody would believe her," said Buckley. "I'm going to reach out, we're going to be friends on Facebook, I'm going to tell this twelve-year-old girl how beautiful she is. She's never heard that before. She's the outcast at school. I'm going to send her gifts in the mail. I'm going to do all these things and tell her all these things she wants to hear. I'm going to make her fall in love with me." Buckley said it's that easy for traffickers and predators to groom vulnerable children.

Traffickers also target kids who are, or were, in foster care. In 2015, almost 30 percent of reported sex trafficking victims younger than eighteen were in foster care, according to Joy. "Children who have aged out of the foster care system have a history of abuse and are more likely to engage in transactional sex," she wrote (103).

Kathy Wilson, Cofounder of the Cullman County (Alabama) Human Trafficking Task Force, tells of a teenage girl who was raised in foster care and was victimized by a sex trafficker. The girl wanted to get a job in the pornographic film industry. "That was her goal. She wanted to do that because she could make lots of money and she thought it was going to be safe," said Wilson.

The girl found an agency online and bought a plane ticket to a state out West. The girl's employer saw the danger and contacted Wilson, who is also a juvenile probation officer, for help. Wilson and others suspected the man was a sex trafficker. They convinced the girl not to go. The same man then asked the girl to fly to a different state for a photo shoot. He bought her a one-way plane ticket. Wilson asked the girl why the man would buy a one-way ticket, explaining how suspicious it sounded. The girl told Wilson the man didn't know exactly how long she would be there, and they did not want to have to re-do a ticket. "The more research we were able to do, the worse it got," said Wilson. "It was horrible. It was a trafficking situation. It was everything that you've ever imagined about somebody who was going to be a victim of human trafficking."

One of Wilson's contacts in law enforcement found solid evidence that the man was running a sex trafficking operation. Wilson texted the evidence to the girl. Again, Wilson, with the help of others, convinced the girl to change her mind. However, the girl found another "modeling agency" online, bought a plane ticket and left without telling anyone. When she had been there about a week, she texted Wilson, saying that everything was great. She was staying in a "modeling house" with another girl and a "modeling mom." Wilson said it was a classic trafficking scenario, but the girl didn't realize it yet. She begged the girl for the address, but the girl refused. "I at least wanted something to be able to tell the police if I never heard from her again," Wilson said. That was, in fact, the last time Wilson ever heard from the girl.

"I was devastated. It was a train wreck," said Wilson. "It broke my heart. She was nineteen years old. And she was a perfect victim, because she's nineteen and she looks like she's twelve. They want somebody that looks like a kid, or is a kid." Wilson said the girl "never really had a life. She was looking for somebody to love her, which is what they're all looking for. Somebody to love them."

Wagar knows another trafficking survivor who grew up in foster care in a large city in the Midwest. The girl's foster parents were inattentive, and she caught the attention of the gang that ruled the block. "It was known that they'll take care of you because the government couldn't do it and other organizations couldn't do it," said Wagar. "But you have to take care of them, and you owe them. And so, at a certain point, she began being sex trafficked by this gang. And it spiraled from there."

EFFECTS OF SEXUAL ABUSE IN CHILDREN

Clearly, not everyone who is sexually abused as a child becomes a sex trafficking victim. But experts show there is a close link between the two. "Here's what we know about our [sex trafficking] survivors. Typically, the majority of them are the victims of childhood physical and-or sexual abuse. If it's not a hundred percent, it's pretty close to it," said Teresa Collier, a Forensic Child Interview Specialist, a trainer for the Child Trafficking Solutions Project, and former Intelligence Analyst for the Alabama Law Enforcement Agency.

Collier said childhood sexual abuse results in trauma, which can appear as depression, guilt, shame or self-blame. "Self-blame is a big one. We see a lot of our adult victim survivors actually taking on blame for things that are happening to them—eating disorders, anxiety, repression, denial, all types of issues that are manifested by the trauma that they've undergone," said Collier.[13]

Adult sex trafficking victims and survivors have trauma that is almost always rooted in childhood, according to Carolyn Potter,

CEO of The WellHouse. "Without exception, if you look at their backgrounds, especially beginning in childhood, you're always going to find abuse and brokenness from early on," said Potter. "I've always known that there's horrific abuse because I have, for the most part, always worked with children who have been abused. But I just never knew how bad it could be until I started working in this."

Penny Billings also works with sex trafficking survivors at The WellHouse, where she volunteers as a mentor and small-group leader. "One thing they seem to have in common is they were sexually abused as children. That seems to be a common denominator with trafficking victims," she said. "Because they're violated at such a young age, they don't know that there are boundaries. So that makes them more vulnerable."

The sexual exploitation of a child can have a profound influence on a person even into adulthood. "When you've got a kid that's been sexually abused from when they were little, or when you've got an adult that was sexually abused as a child, they really haven't had a way to make good choices," said Collier. "Maybe as far as their self-worth is concerned, they think that's all they're good for. Especially if children have adults in their life that aren't protecting them from that kind of thing and, in fact, a lot of times just letting it happen. ... So, our adult victims that come from a background like that, sometimes their only choices are between a bad choice and a worse choice."

Rachel Thomas, M. Ed.,[14] of Houston, Texas, agrees that some people end up being trafficked due to a lack of choices. Thomas is the director of Sowers Education Group and the lead author of *Ending the Game: An Intervention Curriculum for Survivors of Human Sex Trafficking.* She is also a sex trafficking survivor. Thomas frequently meets victims and survivors who think it's their fault that they got trafficked. "And then when we start to peel back the layers, they ran away from an abusive home at fourteen and had a boy-friend that introduced them to this lifestyle. They were surviving," Thomas said. "If you were [underage] and didn't have any of your needs met or were escaping some trauma, you automatically didn't choose this. You may have chosen between two bad options, but you didn't have wonderful options to choose from."

Angela sees the connection between her sexual abuse in child-hood to later being trafficked. She believes that if she had not been exploited and molested as a child, she could have made better choices when she was older. "The role of trauma started as a kid," she said. "I will be honest, the things I saw at five were way worse than when I was an adult. It was so traumatizing that later, like I said, I did all these sexual acts."

Childhood sexual abuse "conditions children from an early age to accept the lies, coercion, false promises and other psychologically damaging behaviors brought to them by traffickers," Joy wrote. She added that adults who were sexually abused as children are far more vulnerable to sex traffickers than people who were never abused. "Their developing brains are often impacted by repeated trauma and have a diminished capacity, or are unable to process new infor-mation, discern danger from safety, control emotion and impulse, and access help" (24-25).

Trauma is well known to cause psychological and physiological problems. "Sexual trauma overwhelmingly can cause PTSD [Post-Traumatic Stress Disorder]," said Wagar. "Having PTSD can open you up to a whole new realm of vulnerabilities that manifest as PTSD symptoms. Prior sexual assault and trauma, that's probably the biggest common denominator."

It's also important to look at long-term trauma, according to Susan Munsey, LCSW,[15] Founder and Director of Programs at GenerateHope in San Diego, California. "We recognize the level of functioning is impacted by complex trauma and that acquisition, not restoration, of some modes of function may be necessary," said Munsey. "So, really looking at that longer-term trauma, we all know that many times we're not just working with the trafficking trauma, but looking back into childhood and the things that may have happened there and the trauma that they brought forward with them from childhood."

The trauma of childhood sexual abuse is not the sole reason that people become trafficking victims, but it frequently is an underlying factor. West helped conduct a study that focused on African American women who all went to the same hospital as children to be treated for sexual abuse. She received a grant that helped her contact some of the women twenty years later as a post-doctoral study. "And what we found was, not only a history of child sexual abuse, but severe child sexual abuse was a big risk factor for later involvement in prostitution and sex trafficking. It also was related to adult sexual violence," West said. "We can't say for certain that child sexual abuse caused that. There were other factors there. What we know is, it can lay a foundation for a trajectory for what we're seeing in prostitution and sex trafficking."

It impairs you for a long time.

ANGELA

| four |

Trauma

'I've been groomed in my mind somehow'

Angela's story in her own words:

Now mind you, they take you to the middle of nowhere, so you have no chances of escaping. You're dependent on this driver for your dear life. You hope he doesn't go eat something and leave you with a total monster. And that's when I first realized, whoa, we're going so far, there's no lights or anything, into these stranger's houses, and pictures of their wives and families are up. I just felt very, "what am I doing?"

I went in like a slave. I just did what I was supposed to. You go in, you have sex with the person, they pay, you leave. Now, I go back to my five-year-old self. I don't say no. I don't know how. I just keep letting myself get exploited now, because I've been groomed in my mind somehow to just don't say no. I don't know why. And so, I hated myself for that. I just hated myself for allowing myself to go with the flow of all these people without ever saying anything.

Angela got out of the life of being trafficked at age eighteen, but her trauma didn't end there. She moved back in with her aunt and uncle. Her story continues below.

So, I stayed with them, and went back to church immediately. They asked me to give my testimony. I started traveling, sharing my testimony all over. Then I went to college, finished four years, still ministering. I still wasn't getting counseling though, that was the big factor. It was a lot of spiritual work, but I hadn't gotten any type of counseling for trauma, for my childhood trauma and PTSD for the things I had to do with these guys. It was just something I just let die down. I went to seminary. I just kept going and going and going for a very long time until I did have a burnout when I finished seminary.

Everything just hit me hard after about eleven years of ministering, helping street kids, helping prostitutes in the streets. I would go to cardboard boxes, where prostitutes were staying. I'll never forget some of these stories. And their pimps only let me talk to them for about five minutes. It's the same thing I experienced, see, but in a different way. Maybe their pimp beats them. That's the kind of damage they do to them. I was more psychologically damaged by these people and their control. But when you talk to them on the streets, these guys will smack them later. He'll beat her. So, I had only five minutes. I can't go over that or she's going to get in big trouble. And then he's kicking me out in maybe even less time. Spitting or yelling. They're pretty crazy. You just never know who made it out and who didn't.

So, I was really busy. I felt like I owed it to people to do as much as I could to help them because of what God had done for me. But in the process, I hadn't really done some of the harder work of healing. I sometimes feel like you never really get over it and you subject yourself to so many people with so many lusts and so many just disgusting habits. You kind of blank out to do them over and over. I just didn't have a way to process it, really. So, I just finally burned out. I started drinking again at twenty-six—a lot—because I was around a lot of Christians who drank a lot. But I had a tendency to depend on it or abuse it. So that kind of came back up in my life after ten years with really no issues with it. That just triggered some things.

I got in trouble with the law again. I was twenty-six years old when I got my first DUI and soon after was charged with a second one. I was in jail for twenty-seven days with three years bench probation, which was terminated early, after only a year. It was a real life-changer. Mind you, I had just finished massive ministry. It was humbling because I had just gotten my master's degree in seminary, and was leading and serving many groups. And then here I am. The shame all came back to me, all over again. Like, oh, you really aren't done with all those past things. Look at you, you're just still the same person covering up.

I had to deal with that and get counseling and really process, and here I am today. That was about thirteen years ago [when she got the DUI]. I still go through many struggles because of [being trafficked]. I'm married, for eleven years now, so it's always something. I have to make sure I don't feel used. I'm just so afraid of being used. That's one of the biggest hurdles in my life, doing ministry. I used to convince myself that I was worth something because I had money from having sex with those men. But it was controlling because they give you this money, then you have to give them [the traffickers] all their fees. And you're kind of like, okay, I'm the one who did all this stuff. I'm the one that put myself in danger in this person's home who I don't know, who probably has guns and weapons in there.

Yeah, those are the problems I still go through with that—not being used, not being taken advantage of, making sure that when I do things I do it with the right motive. And I don't do anything the Lord doesn't ask me to do, because sometimes it's just my mentality once again from childhood. Just serve and serve and give and give until I'm so burned out. And then I go into a bad place. So, I don't know if I'll ever get over that. I've heard other survivors who've overcome this tell me that they think like that too. They always feel used. They have to guard themselves. The person may not even be using you, but you just get the sense that they may be wanting to take advantage of you and exploit you. And that's always there in the back of my mind.

When something triggers me and I get overwhelmed, I definitely will want a drink or something. I want to go back to the agents that help me numb, and that might always be a struggle. No one will look at me and say, oh, she's an alcoholic or a druggie, but I'm always going to feel like any problems I have, have to be secret. And so, I have to have really close friends to talk to and be very honest with. This is hard for me, but they have to be very merciful with anybody who's been through that. Because you don't just get your life together and never have problems again.

Actually, you live your life sometimes getting these overwhelming feelings and wanting to just numb them. That's the only way I can describe it. There's this deep anxiety that comes on me sometimes and I just want to numb everything and so, it's important to talk about it. That's part of where anxiety comes from, not talking about it with anyone. Not letting people know your true story because they can't handle it. That's what I always think, they can't handle it. Only I can, maybe.

* * *

WHAT IS TRAUMA?

Angela, at seventeen, was excited about getting a new job and learning a skill. She didn't understand yet what the job entailed. "There was an ad in the paper for massages. You would think I would know better, but I really did not know," she said. "It turned out to not be massages at all." That first "job" opened the door to a world that Angela didn't know existed. Before long, she was deeply immersed in human sex trafficking, and she didn't know how to get out.

To survive, Angela did what she had to, including drugs. Dr. Joan Gillece describes such behaviors as adaptive symptoms. "Everyone has different adaptations. You might see people that are using [drugs]. Many of the women that I've worked with in the past have told me that when they ended up having sex with someone that they didn't want to have sex with, all it made them do was feel traumatized and use more," said Gillece, Director at the Center for Innovation in Health Policy and Practice in Alexandria, Virginia (a center within the National Association of State Mental Health Program Directors). "So that's symptom as adaptation."

Gillece has worked in the behavioral health field for forty years, including twenty-five years addressing the impact of trauma on trafficking survivors and finding social justice for them. An important part of her approach is to look past the negative. "We're not looking at what's wrong, we're not looking at deficits," she said. "We're here to help you heal and address those symptoms that are adaptive."

In accordance with Gillece's approach, Angela's drug use and having sex with men under coercion were symptoms of her adaption to survive. They were not the root of who she was. Her "going with the flow" of her traffickers is a classic symptom of trauma. She did not want to be in those houses. She did not want to have sex with those men. She deeply experienced the self-hatred and shame that went with it. Her experience lines up with an explanation of trauma as something that "overrides our sense of having a feeling of control, connection and meaning, or being able to make sense of what is happening," according to Dr. Michelle Harrison, founder of Grace to Glory Counseling in Greenville, South Carolina. Harrison is a licensed professional counselor in Kentucky and South Carolina who specializes in trauma and works with women who have been trafficked.

Angela's adaptation to sexual abuse began when she was a child. She learned early that her parents were not her protectors, nor were most other adults. This type of childhood trauma can have a profound effect on the mental health of adults, according to Connie Oden, LICSW,[16] of Birmingham, Alabama.

"Many people who experience abuse develop the core belief that the world is not a safe place. 'I'm helpless. I can't ever do anything right. If only I could make it perfect, everything would be okay.' And those are cognitive distortions at their baseline," said Oden. "If you grow up with abuse and you've got people who violate your boundaries on a regular basis, there are no boundaries. There just are none. So, in keeping with that, you're going to find people with low self-esteem who are going to be very vulnerable to anyone looking for someone to take advantage of."

RISK FACTORS

Sex trafficking victims often have a specific set of vulnerabilities. A major risk factor is being abused sexually as a child, but that's not the only component that makes people more vulnerable. "One of the things that is often overlooked is abandonment," said Oden. An example is children whose parents are addicted to drugs. "They don't abuse their kids, but they're just never there," said Oden. "They're checked out, so these kids wind up raising themselves and are left often to be the victim of people that come into that environment."

Oden said other risk factors can include low self-esteem, self-blame, socioeconomic problems, single-parent households and poverty, among many others. Some of these influences are in play when people choose partners who turn out to be abusers or traffickers. "It's what they're used to. They give off the energy that they need someone who is going to dominate," Oden said. "I have been astounded more and more as I have gone through my career how frequent this is. Abuse is very common."

Another common risk factor is being a runaway. "More than seventy percent of all runaways encounter a child predator within the first forty-eight hours of leaving home," said Amy Joy in *Human Trafficking 101*. The reason, she said, is that many children post on social media that they have left home, giving traffickers the chance to show up and "rescue" the child. "Predators and traffickers know what to look for when it comes to vulnerabilities in people. ... Predators and traffickers know if an individual is worth pursuing based on how a person walks; responds to simple questions; if eye contact is made; or if they appear hungry, thirsty or tired. They can also identify those who are homeless and in need of a place to sleep" (54-55).

Some of the young trafficking survivors at GraceHaven are runaways, according to Jennifer Taber, LISW-S and C-DBT,[17] the Director of Clinical Services and Community Based Programming at GraceHaven in Columbus, Ohio. "As they have become at-risk and needed to provide for themselves, oftentimes there's been an exchange for basic needs that has been provided with sex," Taber said. "From there, that vulnerability continues to lead them further into an exploitative relationship with potentially their trafficker or their exploiter."

Other vulnerable groups are LGBTQ+ people and people of color, both of whom are "more likely to be trafficked than other demographics" (*Polaris* [Recognizing Human Trafficking Vulnerabilities Recruitment]).

LGBTQ+ people can be especially susceptible to sex traffickers because they are sometimes rejected by society and by their families, according to Audrey Baedke, Cofounder and Programs Manager at Real Escape from the Sex Trade (REST) in Seattle, Washington. "We know that there is an intersectionality between members of the LGBTQ community and survivors of the sex trade," said Baedke "First of all, we know that just identifying as LGBTQ makes a person more vulnerable. More vulnerability means more likelihood of entering the sex trade. It makes it harder for people to obtain employment, to obtain housing. Sometimes it means experiencing discrimination among their own family members. And those vulnerabilities make it more difficult for someone to be able to thrive in the mainstream society, and sometimes seek alternative income."

People of color are also frequent targets of sex traffickers. Dr. Carolyn West, Professor of Clinical Psychology at the University of Washington in Tacoma, Washington, specializes in racism in sexualized media and the psychology of Black women, including sexual violence toward Black women. West says at least four types of risk factors affect Black women and girls—individual, relationship, community and societal.

"We know that individual risk factors put young people at risk for trafficking," West said. This includes child abuse; mistreatment; homelessness; sexual orientation; and involvement in the criminal justice, juvenile justice or foster care systems. Relationship risk factors can include family poverty, dysfunction or domestic violence.

Some community risk factors are peer pressure, social norms and social isolation. Societal risk factors include pornography and implicit bias.

"We all know that those things co-occur, but we don't always do a good job of taking all of that into consideration and understanding that people are embedded in these networks," said West. "So [recognizing that is] going to be critical for the work that we do."

West also recognizes that some Black girls and women have a low self-image because of their appearance. "You'll see that in some communities of color," said West. "It's something called colorism, this practice of discriminating based on lighter skin tones being treated more favorably than those with darker skin tones."

In his work, Douglas Gilmer sees vulnerabilities from an entirely different perspective. Gilmer, a federal law enforcement agent in Birmingham, Alabama, who works with human trafficking victims, is most likely to encounter trafficking survivors during sting operations that target traffickers and sex buyers. "The victims of human trafficking are typically all people that have a vulnerability," he said. "Whether it's financial, social, drug dependency, whatever it might be, there's a vulnerability that traffickers are very good at cuing in on. And they're able to exploit those vulnerabilities. That's how they trap people."

Knowing that sex trafficking survivors have been exploited, lawyers Greg Zarzaur of Birmingham and Brian Kent of Philadelphia—who represent sex trafficking survivors in civil court cases— are careful to keep survivors' vulnerabilities in mind. In an anti-trafficking seminar in 2020, the attorneys gave a presentation together where they identified some "pre-existing vulnerabilities" that often lead to someone being trafficked. The most common risk factors they see are substance abuse, runaways (often preceded by sexual abuse in the home) and homelessness. "And so, you have these three things working in conjunction with each other that are just multiplying the vulnerability of that person and making them that much more susceptible to be trafficked," Kent said.

TRAUMA BONDING

One of the hardest things to understand, unless you've been in the situation, is a sex trafficking victim forming a bond with her trafficker. But it happens often.

"I did not expect, nor did I understand in the beginning, the trauma bonding. The fact that they actually have a bond to the people who've abused them so horrendously and who forced them to do things," said Carolyn Potter, CEO of The WellHouse. "It was just always the strangest thing that they would leave and go back to them, or that they would want to continue talking with them. And then we started learning more about Stockholm Syndrome and the reasons behind why they still had a bonding."[18]

Rachel Lloyd, a sex trafficking survivor and founder of Girls Educational and Mentoring Services (GEMS) in New York, describes in her memoir *Girls Like Us* how hard it was for her to leave her abusive pimp. "Viewing pimps as one-dimensional monsters isn't that helpful in terms of understanding the girls' experiences. While the acts that pimps have committed are heinous and deserving of full punishment under the law, overlooking the humanness that the girls surely see only makes it harder to understand why they stay or, especially, why they go back," she wrote. "We understand that women in domestic violence relationships don't necessarily want the relationship to end. They just want the abuse to stop. It's what keeps the cycle going, the belief that this time it will be different, that he'll change, that you can get the good parts back, without any of the bad parts intruding this time (188)."

Amy Wagar, an advocate for Worthy[2] (Worthy Squared) and a trainer for the Child Trafficking Solutions Project, has spent time with trafficking victims who had extreme loyalty to their traffickers. She was once on an undercover operation with the police, in the role of an advocate for trafficking survivors. They were in a hotel room with a woman who was known by police to be a "bottom" (or "bottom bitch" or "bottom girl"), which is a trafficker's trusted person he puts in charge of his other trafficking victims.[19] The woman was running a "circuit," or a specified route.

The woman insisted that no one was forcing her to have sex with men for money. She said she was doing it on her own, despite the evidence in the room. She had a notebook with a list of the cities she had been to and how much money she made from different customers. The police found Western Union receipts where she was sending money back to the state she was being trafficked from. "She kept explicit records," Wagar said. "Page after page after page of money."

Also scattered throughout the room were scraps of paper where someone had handwritten rules for the woman to live by. Wagar picked up one of the papers and asked the woman, "If you're doing this on your own, talk to me about rule number twelve. It says, 'You cannot leave the hotel without permission.' Whose permission do you need?" The woman responded that she meditates and has to give herself permission to leave the room. She never admitted that she was being trafficked. "They all do that," Wagar said. "Because all they know is, protect the pimp, protect 'daddy.'"

Since the woman was working alone, in a different state from her trafficker, it seems like she could have easily left him. "He's a state away. What would make her still do that a state away? You'd think she could escape," Wagar said. "But remember, it's mind control. People often ask, 'Why don't they run? I don't see this person being handcuffed.' But you can't see the chains."

Such scenarios do not surprise Teresa Collier, a Forensic Child Interview Specialist, a trainer for the Child Trafficking Solutions Project, and former Intelligence Analyst for the Alabama Law Enforcement Agency. "You should always pretty much expect affection for and loyalty to their pimp. They typically do have a connection to the person or persons that have been exploiting them," Collier said. "Because honestly, the pimp could be a family member. If it's a male, most likely it's going to be a love-type relationship with the pimp, because that's how they got groomed into that situation, with that individual promising them love and a relationship."[20]

Rachel Thomas, M. Ed.,[21] of Houston, Texas, has experienced the bond herself. Thomas, a sex trafficking survivor, is the director of Sowers Education Group and lead author of *Ending the Game: An Intervention Curriculum for Survivors of Sex Trafficking.* Her trafficker was "physically abusive, psychologically, sexually, spiritually, every form of abusive," said Thomas. He had threatened to kill her and her parents. "When the police got involved, I was uncooperative and I told the police he wasn't that bad."

Thomas said the bonds of attachment are real, "whether it's to a trafficker in the form of a trauma bond or whether it's to the lifestyle itself through identity disturbance. ... So many parts of themselves have been lost or repressed or beaten out of them, that they're operating in a way that is more like a cult victim—somebody that has been mentally manipulated into believing that the lifestyle of commercial sexual exploitation is who they are." She said the bonds don't simply go away when a survivor leaves the life. "It takes work. It takes understanding why those bonds are there," she said.

One of the goals of the *Ending the Game* curriculum is to decrease feelings of attachment to a trafficker or to the lifestyle of commercial sexual exploitation. Thomas recommends survivors start the curriculum soon after leaving trafficking because "the psychological coercion piece is one that causes recidivism." She said recidivism—or going back to the life—is fairly common, especially when survivors first try to leave. She said victims think things like, "I can't do this, I'm going back," or "I still love him, I'm going back."

Thomas said wanting to return to the trafficker is normal, especially at first. She said it's common for survivors to miss their traffickers. "We hear a lot of reasons for the recidivism and why very few survivors get out and stay out on the first try, myself included," Thomas said. "It's normal to doubt you can do this square world thing. This is part of the journey … all these other people in the curriculum feel this way as well."

TRAUMA-INFORMED

A fairly new approach in survivor care—but one that is becoming the standard—is to be trauma-informed. Many organizations that work with human trafficking survivors now use this method. Harrison defines trauma-informed as, "a growing awareness in understanding how trauma impacts a person and informs the lens through which that person perceives themselves, others and the world around them." The approach helps people remember that a survivor's trauma "informs what they think about themselves, what they believe to be true about themselves, others, the world around them, and how it functions."

Before organizations became trauma-informed, Harrison said, a common response to a woman in recovery whose emotions and actions did not fit the situation might be, "What in the world is wrong with you? Stop it." In contrast, she said, trauma-informed care inquires, "What's going on? What from the past is currently impacting you and elicited that response or that behavior?"

Trauma-informed providers understand that the response is a signal that the person has been triggered.

Gillece, who teaches the trauma-informed model to various groups, gives two good examples of how people can learn to implement the model. A female corrections officer who works with juveniles said the girls would bang on their doors at night. The officer thought the girls were being defiant and seeking attention. After Gillece's training, the officer realized the girls bang on their doors at night because bad things had happened to them at night. She decided to try something different.

"So, this wonderful officer, who was pretty hardcore, said, 'You know what I'm going to do at night? I'm going to read them story books,'" Gillece said. "Now, this isn't something we read in a psychiatric journal. This is something that, when she understood the meaning behind that behavior, rather than just writing them up, she came up with her own solution, which I think is brilliant." Gillece later learned that it worked so well, the officer decided to read the girls their school history books out loud at night because some of the girls were unable to sit still in class and concentrate. "Once she started reading it to them, they did a lot better in school," Gillece said.

Her second example is of a male officer in a juvenile justice facility. After he learned about the trauma-informed approach, he decided to paint the cells with softer colors and replace the gray, scratchy blankets with soft fleece blankets.

"It was incredible," Gillece said. "So that's what we really want to see happen, is this kind of revamping of how we understand behavior and then revamping what we do about it ... We want to use not just latex gloves, but kid gloves when we're dealing with the individuals we serve."

Wagar has also learned to treat trafficking victims and survivors with kid gloves. In addition to earning a master's degree in

Crisis Response and Trauma Counseling, Wagar learned to use compassionate care through her advocacy work in the streets of Birmingham, Alabama. "When I first got into this, I expected the very first victim that I worked with to come running up to me, arms open, and say, 'Oh, I'm so thankful that you're here,'" Wagar said, laughing. She was exaggerating, but makes a good point. "That's not how it works. I have been spit on, cussed out, stabbed at, had shoes thrown at me, and told where I can go. You have to have a good understanding of the trauma-informed approach and a victim-centered approach," she said.

Wagar teaches her teams to treat victims and survivors with kindness no matter how the victims react. "There's so much pain and trauma and abuse that's coming out and manifesting right there as a cosmetic effect, and you have to understand what you're looking at and dealing with," she said.

Dr. Stephany Powell said her organization also has to pay careful attention to the victims they work with. Powell, the National Center on Sexual Exploitation's (NCOSE) Executive Director of Law Enforcement Training and Survivor Services in Washington, D.C., said survivors sometimes get attached to her and the NCOSE attorneys. "And sometimes they will do things even if they don't want to do it. And that makes sense, right? Because that's kind of been the mold that they've been used to, especially if they've had a trafficker," said Powell.

She said the organization needs to be "extremely careful" if a survivor is hesitant about pursuing a court case. The staff needs to make sure survivors feel comfortable and safe enough to say if they don't want to proceed with the case. "Isn't that a part of what we're supposed to be doing when we talk about trauma-informed care?" Powell asked.

Kent, the attorney, focuses on being trauma-informed by requiring employees in his firm—including attorneys, paralegals and intake personnel—to be specifically trained to work with survivors and victims of trauma. "That is extremely important, obviously, in these types of cases," said Kent. He said certain aspects of pursuing a court case can trigger trauma for survivors. For that reason, the attorneys often bring in outside experts in human sex trafficking—such as counselors or advocates—to support their clients.

Well-meaning people can unintentionally trigger trauma reactions in sex trafficking survivors by simply talking to them, whether in a conversation or an interview. Shelia Simpkins-McClain, MSSW,[22] Director of Education and Outreach at Thistle Farms in Nashville, Tennessee, is passionate about survivors keeping their stories to themselves until they're ready to share it. Simpkins-McClain, who is also a sex trafficking survivor, said survivors are not obligated to tell their stories. "To be quite honest, everyone loves a good story," she said. "But I don't have to tell people my story. I'm so much more than that."

Simpkins-McClain had negative experiences after telling her story when some media outlets inadvertently re-exploited her. "Back in the beginning, when I first came into the program, we were doing the work before it was called human trafficking," she said. "We actually learned a lot of really hard lessons from it, because, although I believe that they had truly good intentions on wanting to share the work that we do, a lot of news stations took our trauma and sensationalized it."

Simpkins-McClain advises clients who were recently trafficked to keep their stories to themselves until they have healed. She said the staff at Thistle Farms doesn't even know some of their clients' stories, because they don't ask. "We want them to know they don't owe us anything, and to know everything that we do for them is a gift," she said. "It takes a lot of work, a lot of trauma work, to get us in a maintenance stage so that we're not retraumatizing ourselves when we're telling our stories."

Susan Munsey, LCSW,[23] makes a distinction between trauma-informed, trauma-specific and trauma-integrated care.

Munsey, Founder and Director of Programs at GenerateHope in San Diego, California, said the most global of the three is trauma-informed care. "And that would be one that could be used in any kind of a clinical setting, any kind of a program, just so they are coming from a trauma-informed place," said Munsey. "In trauma-informed care, we reconsidered and evaluated all the components of the system in light of the basic understanding of the role that violence plays in the life of our survivors." Two main considerations are avoiding retraumatizing survivors and accommodating their vulnerabilities, according to Munsey.

Trauma-specific services are more explicit. "We recognize that trauma is a defining life event with a complex course that can profoundly shake the victim's sense of self and others. We recognize symptoms as adaptive rather than pathological, so really meeting the survivor where they're at," said Munsey. The primary goals of trauma-specific service are "symptom management, empowerment and recovery."

The trauma-integrated approach is a combination of the two. Trauma-integrated entails "understanding the survivors and their symptoms and the context of their life experience and their history," Munsey said. "There's an understanding of symptoms as attempts to cope." Certain behaviors might have helped survivors cope in the past, but they're no longer working. "So, we need to help them find new coping strategies. ... we're just looking at that big picture. It's a focus on what has happened to the survivor rather than what is wrong with the survivor."

PHYSIOLOGICAL EFFECTS OF TRAUMA

"I'm triggering, Mrs. Amy."

Wagar was painting school classrooms with a group of sex-trafficking survivors when one of the women made that statement. Wagar explained that "triggering" is a Post-Traumatic Stress Disorder (PTSD) response where a stimulus causes a stress or anxiety reaction. "That street was an area where she was trafficked," said Wagar. "Most of these girls have some form of PTSD. I'm not saying there aren't victims that don't have PTSD, I've just not met one." PTSD can cause sex trafficking survivors to be triggered by smells, sounds, words, locations and other events. Wagar slapped her hand onto a table. "That can be a triggering sound from when a pimp slammed the door and beat her. They don't just remember the trauma; they re-experience the trauma."

Angela has been out of sex trafficking for two decades, but she still deals with PTSD. One of her triggers is seeing romantic or sexual scenes in movies or TV shows. "I have to fast forward through the whole part, from kissing to everything. It grosses me out, makes me mad," she said. "I see girls in that situation and I will spend lots of hours thinking about them. I want to save them, of course, but I can't. So, it frustrates me to no end. When I do get those moments, when I think about those girls, life starts overwhelming me."

PTSD can be overwhelming because of the body's response to extreme stress. "Everything you think has a corresponding body response. We don't think something and leave our body back there," said Oden. "Anxiety is a physiological arousal period. It is a body response. And what you must always remember about anxiety, and PTSD as an anxiety disorder, is that stress is cumulative."

Some of Oden's clients are combat veterans who have PTSD. She said they tend to sit rigidly in their chairs, leaning slightly forward. "I know they're beginning to feel more comfortable when they lean back," she said. "If a car goes by outside on the street and backfires, they jump. That hyperarousal is because they're waiting for the next shoe to fall. That is the life of PTSD."

As anxiety increases, the body's responses become more significant. "You get muscle tension that you usually carry in your back and shoulders," said Oden. "Some people, when they get extremely anxious, will have chest pain. And that's why nine out of ten panic attack folks go to the ER with chest pain. It is a panic attack and not angina, which is a serious myocardial infarction." People feel chest pain because small intercostal muscles around the ribs tighten when they experience extreme anxiety, Oden explained. "It feels like you have a girdle on that is being pulled."

Other responses to anxiety include increases in heart rate, blood pressure and hydrochloric acid secretion in the stomach. "That's why high blood pressure is called the silent killer. We don't walk around knowing that our blood pressure is high," Oden said. People also don't realize when their stomach secretes more acid or, often, when their heart rate increases. "All of these symptoms operate underneath your radar. We are intellectual beings, and we don't typically operate with a whole lot of body awareness. And that is to our detriment."

The simple act of breathing can have a tremendous effect physiologically. As anxiety increases, breathing becomes more shallow and rapid. "And again, you won't be aware of it in the moment if you're that anxious," said Oden. The lungs keep oxygen coming in and carbon dioxide going out at a proper balance. The balance of blood gasses is disrupted when breathing becomes shallow in the upper chest. This disruption causes the blood vessels inside the brain to constrict. When the flow of blood, which carries oxygen, is restricted in the brain, the brain can become hypoxic, or have low blood oxygen, Oden explained. "So, you're not going to be able to think clearly. The symptoms exist on a continuum because we breathe twenty-four-seven." At heightened anxiety, people might experience racing thoughts or feel dizzy or lightheaded.

People under extreme anxiety sometimes hyperventilate and faint, which is instructive about the importance of proper breathing. "People faint all the time and think they're going to die. Fainting is not fatal unless you hit your head as you fall down. When you pass out, you're going to start breathing more normally and you're going to wake up," said Oden. "So, that's how important your breathing is to thinking. You can do talk therapy for anxiety for decades, and it will not help if you don't learn to work with your body and your breathing."

At intense levels of stress and anxiety, people sometimes start "just feeling weird," Oden said. "It's called dissociation. That's when you feel disconnected and kind of watching what's going on from above." Collier frequently sees dissociation when she interviews trafficking survivors. "It can be pretty disruptive," she said. The most extreme type is dissociative identity disorder, or multiple personality disorder. "That one is fairly rare," Collier said. "You're not going to see that all the time, but dissociation is on a scale." With less extreme forms of dissociation, Collier said, survivors might break eye contact and stare into space, get tunnel vision, or feel like they're floating.

When Collier sees a survivor experiencing dissociation, she has ways to bring the survivor's mind back to the present. "If you see them disengaging, it's good to ask them about what they're feeling," she said. She will sometimes say, "catch this," and toss them a tennis ball. Or she will have the survivor hold something cold in her hands, go to the bathroom and splash cold water on her face, or stand up and balance on one foot.[24]

Collier has tools to help a survivor snap out of dissociation, but trauma can also affect the brain in permanent ways. "Through research, we know that trauma and toxic stress can actually cause a change in brain architecture. We see fewer neuron connections, and things just aren't connected the way they are with the normal brain," said Collier. "So, at the most basic physiological level, being traumatized means the survivor's brain and body continues to organize itself as if the trauma is still ongoing. So basically, even if nothing really bad is going on, those things work together to defend against a threat that actually started and belongs in the past."[25]

Trauma affects specific areas of the brain, including the hippocampus, amygdala, prefrontal cortex and Broca's area, according to Joy. The hippocampus, which is "partially responsible for properly processing and storing memory, as well as memory recall ... begins to die off and shrink." The amygdala, or the "emotional center of the brain ... becomes overactive when repeated trauma triggers flight, fight or freeze." The prefrontal cortex, which is responsible for "executive decision-making, impulse control and problem-solving," experiences diminished growth. Broca's area, the language center of the brain, has little or no activity during trauma. "If you have ever witnessed someone who has just gone through a horrible event and could not speak, it is because they literally had no words," Joy wrote (106-107).

These brain responses can create chaos in the life of a trafficking victim or survivor. "Trauma, over time, results in poor memory recall, dissociation, personality disorders, depression, anxiety, complex post-traumatic stress disorder, Stockholm Syndrome, substance abuse, diabetes, heart disease, somatic syndrome, and a myriad of other disorders and diseases," Joy wrote (107-108).

Collier points out further results of trauma in victims and survivors. "Some other things that we see caused by traumatic stress are hyper-arousal; poor communication, which goes back to the memory issue and them not being able to assemble memories in a cohesive way; avoidance; negative thoughts and emotions, which do tend to evolve into suicidal ideations; poor health; chronic pain;

and low executive functioning," she said. An example of low executive functioning is when a survivor can never get herself ready and be on time for appointments, or "just not being able to get their stuff together," Collier said.[26]

Of all of the above symptoms, Collier said impaired memory has an especially devastating effect on trafficking victims and survivors. "We have survivors who just have a really hard time sequencing memories or being able to remember what happened a short while ago. They just can't assemble their memory in a cohesive or coherent narrative," she said, adding that this often does not go over well with law enforcement. Police officers sometimes assume that the trafficking survivor is lying, Collier said. "In actuality, it's really something our survivors can't do, physically, because of the neurons that haven't formed in the brain," she added. "They really don't have a way to organize their memories completely."

Impaired memory also has larger implications for trafficking survivors and victims. "Because they can't put all these memories together, so that you have a cohesive type of memory storage, they tend to relive those events over and over again," Collier said. "Those things are triggered by things like smells, images or sounds that resemble the original trauma that started this traumatic stress in the first place."[27]

Collier has a favorite technique to help counteract some of the brain's responses to trauma. During some interviews and in certain court settings, Collier uses courthouse facility dogs, which are trained to work with trauma victims. The dogs are "bred and trained to be non-reactive in stressful situations," said Collier. The dogs also have a physiological effect on victims and survivors. When people experience trauma, they release stress hormones— cortisol and adrenaline—that increase heart rate, blood pressure and breathing rate. "This alters the brain functioning and causes the survival response to kick in," Collier said. "Scientific research indicates that the presence of a dog causes the brain to release oxytocin." The hormone oxytocin counteracts stress hormones by decreasing blood pressure and heart rate. "It allows the fact-finding and reasoning part of the brain to work," Collier said.[28]

VICTIMOLOGY

"Being a victim means having no voice, not able to speak up for oneself," said Oden.

When Angela was being sold for sex as a teenager, she rejected the title of victim. "I would not allow myself to be the victim. That's why I didn't tell anyone my secret story. Because people who have been victimized want to feel like they have some type of control," said Angela. "I wanted to feel empowered and I went about it the wrong way with these people, these men, this secret underground world of escorting and body rubs and whatever they call it. It really is a trap." Angela figured that at least somebody was willing to call her every day and give her money. "'They make me do things that I don't always want to do, but at least I get something out of it.' That was my way of reasoning that I wasn't a victim," she said. "But if you ask me if I was scared, absolutely."

Angela and other sex trafficking victims experience identity shifts, according to Thomas, or "things this person was not born believing, maybe not even raised believing. But once you're in this life, in this world, figuring out how to adapt, how to survive, how to thrive, these are the new beliefs that will take over." Thomas said the new beliefs include things like, "It's better to get paid for sex than to do it for free. Squares are losers. They're boring. They're broke. They're being taken advantage of by the system."

She said trafficking victims' identity shifts encompass the "whole idea of us versus them, and we're superior." Thomas said another new belief is: "The life is as good as my life will get, so I should just make the best of it." She said this belief is especially strong if a victim was abused sexually as a child and she saw herself as a sex object far too young. "There are so many ways that a victim of sex trafficking will tell themselves, 'This is who I am,'" Thomas said.

In other words, *I'm not a victim.*

"It's difficult to view yourself as a victim, no matter what happens to you, when your pimp, the men who buy you, and even those who are supposed to protect you see you as incapable of being victimized," wrote Rachel Lloyd in her memoir *Girls Like Us.* "Prostitution is viewed as a victimless crime, a statement that denies the humanity or victimhood of the women and girls involved (126)."

Sometimes, the title of "victim" is withheld not by the actual victim, but by the community. As Lloyd describes in her memoir, she saw many cases where trafficked teenage girls were not taken seriously. One police officer asked a girl "why she didn't just leave the man who had forcibly kidnapped her." The police told another trafficking victim, who was recruited from Spain and barely spoke English, that they would not charge her rapist because she failed to use the word "force" when she reported the rape at the hospital (125-126).

"Being raped feels just as scary if you're a girl on the track[29] who's been sold to seven men that same night as it does to a 'regular' woman or girl. If you're considered sexually experienced, or even sexually active, the degrees of harm done by sexual assault are often measured out according to your level of 'culpability,'" Lloyd wrote. "While this view isn't limited to girls in the sex industry and is often imputed to victims of sexual violence who are considered promiscuous, women and girls in the sex industry are obviously seen as the least affected by sexual violence" (125-126).

Lloyd is describing implicit biases toward sex trafficking victims. West defines implicit biases as "those assumptions, stereotypes and unintended actions either positive or negative that we make toward others based on race, religion, age, gender and sexual orientation." West said implicit biases are "stored in our subconscious, and we may act on them and not even be aware that we're acting on them." Other times, biases "aren't even implicit, some of them are very intentional. And that's another painful conversation," she said.

Implicit bias is a reason that Black girls and women are "more likely to be trafficked because, oftentimes, people don't see them as victims," West said. She cited a study by Georgetown Law Center where researchers asked, "What are your perceptions of Black girls as opposed to White girls?" The questions were about girls ages five to fifteen. The study found that "adults perceived Black girls as needing less nurturing, needing less protection, needing to be supported less, needing to be comforted less, more independent, knowing more about adult topics, and knowing more about sexuality-related issues," said West. She said the perception is that Black girls and women are "strong, they can take care of themselves, maybe they're even more violent, and not as vulnerable as girls of other backgrounds."

Race-based implicit biases are common, as are biases toward people who make "bad choices" that result in bad outcomes. Collier said people tend to judge trafficking victims who believed a trafficker's lies when he promised her a better life. "Some people say, 'Why would they fall for something like that?" Collier said. "Well, there's a really good reason why a lot of people fall for that type of thing. A lot of victims are just searching for what they never had in childhood. They all want somebody to love them and they want to be safe. They just want a life like the rest of us have, and they're searching for that. But you have these master manipulator traffickers out there that promise them those things, and at the end, it's not really what they were promised. It's a lot worse than what they were promised."

Collier said you have to understand victimology to realize why people fall for scams and lies. "It's because they're desperately searching for a better life and somebody to love them and those things that they never had as kids," she said. "It fits like a glove why it seems like our trafficking victims so easily fall victim to that crime. It's mostly because of their past victimization as children. It does irreversible damage to a person's psyche when they're sexually abused as children."

Victimology is also a reason trafficking cases are difficult to prosecute, according to Collier. (There is more about this in Chapter 5.) "It's because you have victims that don't always identify as victims. In fact, most of the time they don't identify as victims," said Collier. Victims and survivors are not likely to testify against their traffickers when they blame themselves for being trafficked. And without witness testimony, prosecutors have a hard time making a case against traffickers.

It can take a really long time for a survivor to
feel comfortable coming forward
or to engage in litigation like this.

DANI PINTER

| five |

Law

'I'm actually going into a jail cell'

Angela's story in her own words:

One day he [Angela's former boss at the massage business] said, "I'm going to Cancun." Although he had other girls, he said, "Can you come and be here and kind of take charge of everything?" And I was like, "Oh, sure." I get to stay in his condo. It would give me a little break from the escorting, even though they call me all the time so I felt an obligation to be there, even though there was really no obligation except fear.

And so, I went to his house to help with this other girl. I didn't know there was a girl there fourteen years old. She looked like she was twenty-five. She looked so big. She's got really big breasts, just a big grown-up body. And she was working. She lied to him, same thing as me, fake ID.

So, I'm overseeing everything. And I told her one day the same thing he schooled me on. If anybody asks you, "How much money?" say, "We already discussed that on the phone." Don't tell them a payment amount.

Don't say, "I will do this stuff to you for this much." That means it's an exchange and you can go to jail.

So, we just happened that day to get a knock on the door from one of the clients. And he kind of looked like a cop, to be honest. I should have known. But I had never been to jail or in trouble like that with the law, so I didn't know any better. He kept saying, "Oh I just got my taxes, so I can pay for a lot of things. What would you do?" And I'm like, "We already told you, a body massage." And he kept on and the girl said, "Oh sure, for that much I'll do this."

Boom, he had it recorded. And immediately he got dressed and left. We heard boom, boom, boom, boom, boom. It was a total sting. And the people in that building for years have been collecting information. They've been telling the cops, "There are all these men coming in and out, of all types of backgrounds, religious men, all types. They're going to this apartment over and over. We think something might be up." So, the cops were already collecting information.

So, all these undercover cops rush in. And it's just me and this fourteen-year-old. I was eighteen, so I'm just at that legal age where I get prosecuted as an adult, I believe. I wasn't even sure. But I think that they're going to be really harsh on me when they found out her age, because they separate you right away. They took us in handcuffs to jail. I left the building in handcuffs. They looked through my purse, my stuff, they looked through his house and found money. They took all that money. They took my money. They found some cocaine and weed and things like that.

So, immediately, they had this whole report. I went right to jail. You walk through those doors for booking, there's people saying they're going to snatch your chain, good luck to you, they're yelling from the cells. I'm freaking out, like, "I'm actually going into a jail cell." I just never put into my mind that what I was doing could really get me in trouble.

So yeah, I went to jail. They asked me for my information and they called my mother to verify, and then that was it. They let me out that next morning with a court date. So, I took that paper and I hid it in my house where my boyfriend lived, and he found that paper. And that's when we got in the biggest fight ever. He started calling me a prostitute and all this stuff. He just flipped on me and I just had no recourse.

I called my mom, and I was really scared because now I didn't know if I was going to go to jail for a long time. I just really didn't know what happens at this point.

And, I guess if you want to know how I got out of the life, it's the going to jail. That's when I realized that if I ever got caught again, it's not these guys that are going to get in trouble, it's me that's going to get in trouble.

* * *

TRAFFICKING LAWS IN THE U.S.

Angela was arrested and jailed because the police didn't realize she was a trafficking victim. Her trafficker had made her a "bottom," or a trusted person put in charge of other trafficking victims (see more about this in Chapter 4). Her traffickers had successfully used psychological coercion to make her believe that she was not a victim and that she was making her own choices. Like Angela, countless victims of human sex trafficking are not only exploited, but end up in jail as a result. For many years, the law was not on their side. The law didn't support their status as victims. That changed more than two decades ago, with the Trafficking Victims Protection Act. The

TVPA made some positive changes, but it did not even come close to eliminating human sex trafficking in the United States.

TVPA

In 2000, Congress passed the Trafficking Victims Protection Act (TVPA) to address sex trafficking and labor trafficking. The TVPA is a subsection of the Victims of Trafficking and Violence Protection Act of 2000.

The TVPA criminalized two major forms of human trafficking —labor and sex trafficking. "Before that, if you wanted to prosecute somebody for what we now call human trafficking, you would have to show force or some abuse of the law in order to prosecute someone for that crime," said Gregory Zarzaur, a trial lawyer at Zarzaur Law Firm in Birmingham, Alabama. However, the TVPA changed that. "In 2000, Congress recognized that the crime of human trafficking has become more nuanced now and there are ways vulnerable people are controlled that may not necessarily amount to the traditional use of force," Zarzaur said.

TVPA Section 102(b)(1) states some of Congress's findings about human trafficking: "As the 21st century begins, the degrading institution of slavery continues throughout the world. Trafficking in persons is a modern form of slavery, and it is the largest manifestation of slavery today..."("Victims of Trafficking And Violence Protection Act"). Human trafficking, often called modern-day slavery in the anti-trafficking world, happens in every country.

The TVPA mandates that the U.S. Department of State must publish an annual report that ranks countries on their human trafficking policies and what they're doing to eliminate trafficking. This annual publication is called the Trafficking in Persons (TIP) Report. More than 175 countries contributed information for the 2021 TIP Report (24). In addition to statistics about specific countries, the

2021 version includes information about familial trafficking, the danger of trafficking misinformation, state-sponsored trafficking and much more.

The TIP Report breaks down what the TVPA actually means for sex trafficking survivors by using the *Action-Means-Purpose* model (26-27). For an incident to be classified as human sex trafficking, one item from each category must be present. "All three elements are required to establish a sex trafficking crime (except in the case of child sex trafficking where the means are irrelevant)," the report states (26).

The anti-trafficking organization Polaris explains the Action-Means-Purpose model this way: "Human trafficking occurs when a perpetrator, often referred to as a trafficker, takes an *Action*, and then employs the *Means* of force, fraud or coercion for the *Purpose* of compelling the victim to provide commercial sex acts or labor or services" (*Polaris* [Understanding Human Trafficking]).

The TVPA's Action-Means-Purpose model is further explained below, using examples compiled from the TIP Report and from Polaris.

Action

Perpetrators can take numerous actions toward sex trafficking victims, such as inducing, recruiting, harboring, transporting, providing, obtaining, patronizing or soliciting. Amy Joy writes in *Human Trafficking 101* that "[a]ny person found to be conducting any of these activities in conjunction with the purpose of [exploitation] can be convicted of a human trafficking crime." She gives the example of a trafficker asking his mother to watch over two teenage victims while he runs errands. The trafficker's mother "is now part of the human trafficking chain and can be charged with harboring two victims of sex trafficking" (20).

In Angela's case, many people were involved in trafficking her. Someone placed the fraudulent ad that drew her to the illicit massage business. A "friend" recruited her into escorting. Drivers transported her to countless men's homes and hotel rooms for sex. However, as is typical, none of those people were around when Angela was arrested

Means

Traffickers use at least one of three means described in the TVPA: force, fraud or coercion.

The first means, *force*, is "exactly what it seems," wrote Joy. "It means that someone has been or is being physically taken and/or held against their will as well as beaten, raped and/or tortured to keep them from being free" (18). Angela's traffickers forced her to complete her "dates," even when she told them she felt uncomfortable and didn't want to continue.

The second means, *fraud*, is "basically tricking someone. A trafficker promised one thing ... and delivered something completely different," said Joy (18-19). In Angela's case, the massage business and the escort service both used fraud by misrepresenting what the jobs actually entailed.

Coercion, the third means, is "often referred to as the process of 'boy-friending' or 'grooming,'" Joy wrote (19). Coercion consists of "mind games" or inducing someone to do something against their will without using physical force. Angela's traffickers used coercion by making her think she was choosing to be a prostitute and by threatening that she, and not them, would be put in jail if she got caught. On this, they were right. They also put fear into her: she thought her traffickers would kill her if she stopped working for them.

The means of force, fraud or coercion is often direct and clear. At other times, those methods are more nuanced. The TIP Report states that means can "include serious harm, psychosocial harm, reputational harm, threats to others, and debt manipulation" (27). Minors are an exception to this section of the model. The TVPA states that the presence of force, fraud or coercion is irrelevant if a minor is trafficked. Any commercial sex act with a person under the age of eighteen violates the TVPA. "If there is a child being exploited through pornography, a strip club, sold online for sex, or any other commercial sex act, they are automatically considered victims of human trafficking and entitled to all the same services and protections as any other victim," wrote Joy (21).

Purpose

The TVPA states two overall purposes of human trafficking: commercial sex (sex trafficking) and labor or services (labor trafficking). Joy writes that the purposes can include exploitation, involuntary servitude, forced military service or debt bondage (15-16). In Angela's case, the purpose was sexual exploitation. According to the TIP Report, "[s]ex trafficking can take place in private homes, massage parlors, hotels, or brothels, among other locations, as well as on the internet" (27).

As for labor trafficking, the report states, "[t]here is no limit on the location or type of industry. Traffickers can commit this crime in any sector or setting, whether legal or illicit, including but not limited to agricultural fields, factories, restaurants, hotels, massage parlors, retail stores, fishing vessels, mines, private homes, or drug trafficking operations." The report further states that two of the most widespread forms of labor trafficking are domestic servitude and forced child labor (26).

TVPRA

Congress has revamped the TVPA several times, beginning in 2003, and renamed it the Trafficking Victims Protection Reauthorization Act (TVPRA).

Among other changes, the TVPRA helped open the door for civil lawsuits by offering "a civil remedy for those who have been trafficked against those who knowingly financially benefitted," said Dani Pinter Esq., Senior Legal Counsel at the National Center on Sexual Exploitation Law Center. "So not only can a survivor sue their trafficker, but they can sue anyone that knowingly financially benefitted, or should have known that they were financially benefitting."

Zarzaur noted that the original TVPA, passed in 2000, did not include a civil remedy for the survivor. "But in 2003, Congress, I think, recognizing the enormity of the issue as it relates to human trafficking and how can we best combat this, added another tool, another resource, another weapon in the fight against human trafficking. And they added a civil remedy provision to what they now call the TVPRA."

A good summary of the updated versions of the TVPRA is at the Alliance to End Slavery and Trafficking website.

FOSTA-SESTA

Another law aimed at fighting trafficking in the United States is nicknamed FOSTA-SESTA, passed by Congress in 2018. The actual names of the bills are the Allow States and Victims to Fight Online Sex Trafficking Act (FOSTA) and the Stop Enabling Sex Traffickers Act (SESTA). FOSTA is the U.S. House of Representatives bill and SESTA is the U.S. Senate bill.

The purpose of FOSTA-SESTA was to amend the Communications Decency Act, Section 230, which basically deemed that websites would not be held responsible for content put there by others. Human traffickers were able to exploit victims online, with no consequence to the website host. An example is the former business Backpage, which allegedly operated a website that allowed traffickers to illegally sell people for sex, including children. In 2018, after the passage of FOSTA-SESTA, the company's chief executive "pleaded guilty to state and federal charges stemming from a wide-ranging investigation into the sex ad website," according to Reuters (Whitcomb).

The Communications Decency Act, Section 230, was the reason that "Internet actors have been able to get away with so much for so long, because there's been this broad immunity applied to the Internet," said Pinter. Many trafficking victims paid the consequences of websites not being held responsible for content posted on them. Pornography websites and websites that sold people for sex refused to remove photos or videos even after the victims reported that they were minors or reported they did not give their permission for their images to be uploaded, according to Pinter.

Big Internet companies made tremendous profits off of those photos and videos. "They were banking on that immunity," said Pinter. "FOSTA-SESTA now allows trafficking survivors to bring claims against Internet companies that have benefited from their abuse. So, we really want to use that law. And we want to use it to change society and bring a measure of justice to victims if possible."

PAGE ACT

The TVPA is technically not the first anti-human-trafficking law in the United States. The federal government has recognized for almost 150 years that prostitution and human trafficking is happening within its borders (not even considering the United States' horrific institution of legalized slavery as human trafficking, which it was). "Our first restrictive immigration law in the United States was also our nation's first anti-human-trafficking law," said Douglas Gilmer, a federal law enforcement agent in Birmingham, Alabama, who works with human trafficking victims. "It was called the Page Act of 1875. We've been looking at this for over one hundred and forty-five years from a legal standpoint in the United States."

Congress enacted the Page Act following an influx of Chinese men and women into the United States in the second half of the nineteenth century. The Act criminalized the bringing of Chinese and certain other Asian immigrants to the United States against their will and forcing them into servitude. It also prohibited bringing Asian immigrants to the U.S. for "lewd and immoral purposes" and it "'explicitly forbid' the importation of women for the purposes of prostitution," according to History.com. The Page Act effectively forbad the immigration of Chinese women to the United States (Rotondi). The Act, however, did nothing for trafficking victims in the twentieth century or for American victims, ever.

TRAFFICKING SURVIVORS AND THE LAW

What effect does anti-trafficking laws have on actual trafficking victims and survivors?

Soon after the TVPA became law in 2000, the United States was shocked by terrorism, and human trafficking was again a low priority. "Right after the federal law was passed, we had 9-11," said Teresa Collier, a Forensic Child Interview Specialist, a trainer for the Child Trafficking Solutions Project, and former Intelligence Analyst for the Alabama Law Enforcement Agency. "So then, a large part of federal law enforcement training and everything else went to the development of Homeland Security and fighting terrorism at home. So, trafficking sort of took a backseat to all that until the end of the decade."

In 2009, Collier finally started seeing more federal anti-sex-trafficking training for state and local law enforcement. As a result, law enforcement agents today are more sensitive to the plight of sex trafficking victims and survivors. Many agencies conduct undercover operations to target buyers and traffickers, and to help victims. Even so, sex trafficking victims continue to end up on the wrong side of the law, especially victims of color.

"Human trafficking victims are often arrested for acts they were forced to commit by their traffickers. And ... human trafficking victims are rarely identified as such at the time of arrest or prosecution," said Jessica Emerson, Director of the Human Trafficking Prevention Project at the University of Baltimore School of Law in Baltimore, Maryland.

A 2016 survey by the National Survivor Network "came up with some truly startling results" about sex and labor trafficking, said Emerson. Ninety-one percent of the network's survivors said they had been arrested. Of those, 42 percent were arrested as minors. "Over 50 percent of the respondents reported every single arrest on their criminal record was trafficking-related," Emerson added. "Over 40 percent were arrested nine or more times. So, we're not talking about one or two arrests. We're talking about incredibly large criminal records that have incredible impacts on survivors." She said 60 percent of those surveyed were arrested for crimes other than prostitution. "And 80 percent reported that they did not disclose their victimization at the time of their arrest, either because they were scared to, because their trafficker told them not to, or simply because no one asked them. So, again, we are talking about an epidemic of arrests of survivors and the opposite of an epidemic in terms of identifying these individuals as such at the time of their arrest or prosecution."

Sometimes the criminal justice system inadvertently forces people to continue in trafficking or prostitution. Glen Buckley, founder of 731 Rescue and the Scarlet Rope Project, recalls a woman he arrested a few years ago when he worked as a law enforcement officer. She was released from jail on bond, and he arrested her again two weeks later. The second time, the woman told him she really wanted to quit prostitution and make a new life. "She said, 'But I had to go out and make the money to pay the court cost from the last time you arrested me,'" said Buckley. "So, here you have somebody who really wanted to get out. She had to make money and survive the only way she knew how." Buckley said the problem was that the court system did not see such women as victims. "All we were doing was arresting them, putting them into the system and creating more problems for them, because now they've got a court cost. They've got to go out and turn more tricks to pay for the fines at court. Nobody was identifying them as victims and figuring out a way to end that cycle."

Even after a trafficking survivor is released from jail or probation, the effects of the arrest linger in the form of criminal records. Having a record can have far-reaching impacts for trafficking survivors. "Criminal records can prevent survivors from obtaining employment, from receiving housing assistance, from pursuing their education, obtaining public benefits, applying for credit or loans," Emerson said. "Criminal records can impact a survivor's family stability, access to immigration relief or to be able to adjust their status."

Angela's criminal record showed up later in life and kept her from getting a job. She didn't have to go back to court or to jail on the solicitation charge when she was eighteen because when she called to find out the status of her case, the docket number was listed as closed. However, years later she applied for a job in senior care. When the company sent in Angela's fingerprints for a background check, the soliciting charge popped back up. Although it has been more than twenty years since the charge, which was dropped, Angela still has this problem anytime she has to be fingerprinted.

Arresting trafficking survivors like Angela violates the very law that the government implemented to protect them. The TVPA, in addition to defining human trafficking, states that "victims of severe forms of trafficking should not be inappropriately incarcerated, fined or otherwise penalized solely for unlawful acts committed as a direct result of being trafficked," Emerson said. Despite the TVPA, survivors sometimes feel more like criminals than victims, especially if they have served time in jail. "And so, the bottom line ... is that a criminal record often keeps survivors trapped in the very industries they seek to escape, prevents their healing, and makes them vulnerable to revictimization," Emerson added.

Carolyn Potter, CEO of The WellHouse, said her clients sometimes have to deal with previous arrests while trying to recover from their trafficking experiences. "Unfortunately, we've had young ladies with warrants and they've been picked up. They've had to go to jail," said Potter. "We just had one recently this happened to. She could not even remember being charged. And she had warrants all over the state. She finally was able to leave jail and come back to us. We visited her, we accepted her phone calls. We just reassure them that we're there for them."

Gilmer said his federal law enforcement agency, which he was not authorized to name in this book, takes a victim-centered approach and, thus, tries not to arrest victims. "Because you're punishing the victim over something they don't have a choice over. So typically, we try very hard not to arrest victims," Gilmer said. The exception is when the victim has warrants. "We are bound by law to execute that warrant," he added. "We don't have a choice. We can't just let that person go if they have an outstanding felony warrant. So, there are those extreme cases. But we try very hard to avoid that." He added that when trafficking victims do get arrested for prostitution, it is usually by state or local agencies because prostitution is a state crime. "It's typically a misdemeanor. We don't enforce state misdemeanors," Gilmer said.

Not all law enforcement agencies, however, take a victim-centered approach. Collier worked for several years training law enforcement officers about human sex trafficking. She said awareness has come a long way, but there is still work to do. "You still have some law enforcement that just don't believe in sex trafficking. They look at any type of commercial sexual activity as prostitution," Collier said. In her classes, police officers sometimes tell Collier that they simply don't believe some victims. "They think with some victims, their bad choices are the reason they're in the situation they're in. So, we still have law enforcement that think that way."

Gilmer said it's "not just about putting people in handcuffs and taking people to jail. That does happen," he said. "There are still departments in the country that probably have a kind of an old-school approach to this. And that's unfortunate. But I think that's also another avenue in which well-trained advocates and victim-service providers can help educate law enforcement, as well. And really get them to see the benefit of working with victim service providers."[30]

Wagar is one anti-trafficking advocate that works with law enforcement. I recently sat in on a training session where Wagar was teaching police officers about human sex trafficking. I saw how officers and detectives in some police departments use condescending language about prostitution and sex trafficking. The men and women in the class were sharing stories about their encounters with sex workers. One of the men told Wagar about going on "hooker patrol" with his team. Wagar stopped him. "Did you just say *hooker patrol?*" she asked. She put her hand over her heart. "These are my people!" Wagar said. She asked the man if he knew that up to eighty percent of prostitutes on the streets are actually being forced there by someone else, meaning they are sex trafficking victims. "I've never met a single prostitute or trafficking victim that said when she was a little girl, 'I want to be a prostitute when I grow up,'" Wagar told the class.

Collier said she sees hope with the next generation of law enforcement leaders having more awareness of sex trafficking. "What I hope is, all the young guys that we can train, and really get them to understand about the victimology of trafficking, those guys within the next ten years or so will be in those higher management positions where they can start making some decisions. I think over the next ten years, we're going to see a lot more being done at the local level, as far as investigating [sex trafficking] cases," she said.

Awareness and education are necessary for everyone in the criminal justice arena. Collier said it takes time for prosecutors and judges to get familiar with new laws. The state of Alabama passed human trafficking legislation in 2010, being the forty-fourth state to do so. "That really wasn't that long ago. It takes a while for prosecutors to get comfortable with the new law, to get comfortable with making charges or allowing their police officers to make those charges," Collier said. Even so, the state has seen an increase in the number of human trafficking charges filed since the legislation passed.

State and federal legislation does work, even if it takes time. "The wheels of justice turn slow," said Kathy Wilson, Cofounder of the Cullman County (Alabama) Human Trafficking Task Force. In that county, Wilson has seen an increase of human trafficking cases since the state law passed. On the federal level, Gilmer also reports an increase in trafficking cases. "It's actually a very big percentage of the work that we do here in Alabama, particularly the Birmingham and Montgomery area," said Gilmer. "About fifty-six percent of our case hours for this past year [2019] have been dedicated to human trafficking investigations."[31]

PROSECUTING: 'A PERFECT STORM'

Getting a successful prosecution for a human sex trafficking charge is notoriously difficult. Several factors contribute to why it is so hard, but one of the main reasons is that victims and survivors are reluctant to testify.

"This is a low-risk crime. It is high profits, low risk because these victims are so traumatized that they won't come forward. No victim, no crime," said Lt. Darren Beams of the Tuscaloosa (Alabama) Police Department and founder of the West Alabama Human Trafficking Task Force. When Beams ran the department's vice unit, investigators discovered twenty-nine confirmed sex trafficking victims, along with a few women who were working as prostitutes with no trafficker.

"Twenty-nine victims. And do you know how many prosecutions we had?" Beams said. "Zero. They wouldn't prosecute them. One reason is, the victims wouldn't come and sit in that witness box and say, hey, this is what happened to me."

Beams has come close to getting sex trafficking cases prosecuted. "I had one defendant—it was a beautiful case. I had the evidence. I had the ads. I had the text messages on her phone where he was saying, 'check your door, you have another client.' And then I had him telling his brother on a jail-recorded conversation to, 'go find that girl and put your foot on her throat where she won't testify.'

And she didn't. But, do I have enough right there to prosecute him without that victim sitting in that witness box? Not in this state."

Beams had another solid case with two sex trafficking victims who refused to testify, but for different reasons. One of the victims was nineteen and had been trafficked since she was twelve. The other victim, who had the same trafficker, was twenty-six. She had met their trafficker at a strip club. Both of the women were from another state but were being trafficked in Tuscaloosa.

A few years passed since the trafficker's arrest. Beams explained that in Tuscaloosa County, human trafficking is a felony that takes an average of three-and-a-half to five years to get to court because the defense attorneys and prosecutors file numerous motions.

"Three-and-a-half to five years is a long time," said Beams. In that time, the trafficker bonded out of jail and the victims took separate routes.

The younger victim "gets her life together," said Beams. She went to college, got a good job and had a child. "Her life has moved on and she's not going to talk about selling her body three or four years ago. She doesn't want to come testify despite the fact that she gave you a real good recorded statement," Beams said. Meanwhile, the older victim went right back to the trafficker as soon as he got out of jail.

"So, you've got one that's not coming back [as a witness against the trafficker] because she's moved on with her life, and you've got one that's not coming back because she's still working for him," said Beams. "So, the traffickers know that it's high profits and low risk."

Cases like that are common. The Trafficking in Persons (TIP) Report has shown an overall increase in the identification of human trafficking victims worldwide in recent years, but the number of prosecutions in trafficking cases is not keeping pace (60).

However, the figures do not necessarily represent a complete picture, according to Gilmer. He pointed out that prosecutors often use another strategy: charge traffickers with something besides human trafficking.

"While I know that the number of victim identifications is up, the number of prosecutions *appears* to be down," said Gilmer. "They're [the TIP Report] only looking at prosecutions for the substantive charge of human trafficking. And a lot of times, we never prosecute on the actual human trafficking charge."[32]

Gilmer agrees that getting a conviction for the actual charge of human trafficking is difficult because victims often do not want to serve as witnesses. Sometimes, they are too traumatized to testify, according to Gilmer. "I don't mean this in a bad way, but survivors are typically the weakest link in a case. And because of physical and emotional trauma, a lot of them are just not stable enough to testify," he said. "And even if they are, why do we want to re-victimize, retraumatize somebody by putting them on a stand where they're going to face a hostile defense attorney who's going to pick apart every part of their life, everything that they've ever done, and is going to call them names and cast them in a very ugly light? Especially when we're trying to help this person."[33]

Potter sees this from the survivors' point of view. Resident survivors at The WellHouse are often reluctant to testify against their traffickers. "It takes a lot to prosecute a trafficker. You need the cooperation of the victim. She needs to be willing to testify against them and to tell her story," Potter said. But many victims are unwilling to do so, she added, because they are afraid that the trafficker might not be convicted. If that happens, the trafficker will possibly come after them, their children or other loved ones. "And they should be fearful of that," Potter said. "These are scary people. They do horrible things to people."

For these reasons, law enforcement personnel often charge human traffickers with crimes that are easier to prosecute. "There are other charges out there we can use that are related to human trafficking that don't require victim testimony," said Gilmer. One charge is the Mann Act, "which is the transportation of individuals across state lines for the purposes of prostitution," said Gilmer. "All we have to do is show that they transported individuals from one state to another."

However, traffickers often do not take their victims across state lines. Law enforcement can also use a Racketeer Influenced and Corrupt Organization (RICO) charge if traffickers commit a crime that impacts interstate commerce. "It could be the use of a cell phone or the use of a computer to transmit information. We can use those violations," Gilmer said.

He added that traffickers can also be charged on money laundering, gun or drug offenses. "I think that's the trend that you're starting to see more and more of at this point. Because we can get the same outcome by putting the person in jail under these other charges without having to retraumatize the victim on the stand," said Gilmer.[34]

In her former work at the Alabama Law Enforcement Agency, Collier often saw traffickers get charged with crimes other than trafficking. "A lot of the cases get investigated and charges pled down to something else like rape or promoting prostitution, when actually there are very high indicators that it's trafficking and not just prostitution," Collier said. "They might get pled down to something else because it will be easier to prosecute."

Collier saw this happen after she interviewed a sixteen-year-old girl who had been sold and raped. The girl saw her rapist hand money to her cousin. "She said to her cousin, 'Did you just sell me to him?'" said Collier. The girl was trafficked, but the prosecutor told Collier it was easier to charge the man with rape than it would be to educate a jury on what human trafficking is. "So that's kind of the mindset that you find a lot with our local prosecutors and state prosecutors. They're still just not comfortable. They can try a rape charge all day long and make it stick, because they know how to do that. They've done a ton of those cases."

Prior to Congress passing the TVPA in 2000, human trafficking was often prosecuted as something else entirely, according to Wilson. "We have had human trafficking forever. It's just been called something else before, like child abuse," she said.

Sometimes the actual law gets in the way of prosecuting traffickers, according to Collier. In Alabama, anyone under the age of nineteen is considered a juvenile in a human trafficking case. This makes prosecuting a sex trafficking case easier, because prosecutors do not have to prove force, fraud or coercion as they do in adult trafficking cases. However, in Alabama, the age of consent for sex is sixteen years old. "Let's put it in perspective," said Collier. "If you have a sixteen-year-old that gets recovered in an undercover op where they are being prostituted out by somebody, the age of consent is sixteen. So, that kid might not disclose that they were being forced. Then law enforcement is not going to try to make a case because the age of consent is sixteen. And that is just a bunch of bull. How many sixteen-year-olds do you know that can make a good decision like that?"

All of these factors contribute to the difficulty of prosecuting human sex trafficking. Collier calls it "a perfect storm of different things of why a prosecutor might not want to go to trial with a sex trafficking case."

Gilmer does not expect changes in the system anytime soon. "Until the law changes and it allows us to be able to prosecute these cases without having to physically put that person on the stand, I think you're going to see that trend continue," he said. "We already do it with minors. If we could do it with adults, I think we'd be much more successful at those substantive violations. So just because the

[TIP Report] numbers don't reflect an increase, it doesn't mean that the prosecutions aren't happening. They're happening. They're just happening with other charges."[35]

As Potter points out, traffickers often are committing additional crimes anyway. "It's not just human trafficking," she said. "It's usually substance abuse, drug trafficking, guns, other kinds of violence, theft. There's usually so many other things wrapped up in this crime. And so, it would seem to me that if you get a trafficker off the streets, then you've resolved a lot of issues, not just solely the issue of human trafficking."

CRIMINAL VERSUS CIVIL

The 2021 TIP Report highlights the difficulty of prosecuting trafficking cases criminally. The report states that 109,216 sex trafficking victims were identified worldwide in 2020 (excluding fourteen countries that did not participate in reporting). Of those, only 9,876 sex trafficking cases were prosecuted, resulting in 5,271 convictions (60). This means that in 2020, only 9.04 percent of reported victims saw their traffickers prosecuted, with 4.83 percent seeing their traffickers convicted on charges of sex trafficking.

However, criminal prosecution is not the only route for survivors to find justice. Another legal option is civil court. Here are the basic differences in criminal and civil litigation:

Criminal

In the criminal justice system, a trafficker is criminally prosecuted for violating the law. His or her guilt or innocence is determined by a jury, a judge or a guilty plea. If the trafficker is found guilty, he or she could be sentenced to jail or prison. The burden of proof is "beyond a reasonable doubt." This standard is "the highest burden we have under our legal system here in the United States," said Zarzaur.

Civil

The civil justice realm is a separate entity from criminal justice. Here, no crimes are charged. Nobody goes to jail. Instead, the victim sues for money (compensation for injury) or for policy changes. The burden of proof is lower than for criminal cases. The burden of proof is "a preponderance of the evidence," or in other words, "more likely than not," Zarzaur said.

As explained earlier, the 2008 revision to the TVPRA was important for the expansion of civil litigation. "The original version allowed the survivor to file a claim against their trafficker, and it was relatively limited in its ability to be used by a survivor," said Zarzaur. "But in 2008, Congress amended the civil remedy to add that anyone who knew or should have known they received anything of value could be sued by the survivor under the 2008 amendment to the TVPA. So, in my opinion, in 2008 it opened the door."

Zarzaur said one particular phrase in the 2008 version is key. "It's that *should have known* language that I think kicked open the door," Zarzaur said. That phrase asks what *should* an individual or business have known was going on within their realm of operation. Potential civil defendants could include hotels, truck stops, financial companies, brands, websites, technology companies or other entities.

In other words, civil litigation is a way to hold everyone accountable that enables traffickers, according to Brian Kent, an attorney with Laffey, Bucci and Kent, LLP, of Philadelphia. "And Congress, thankfully, has said, 'If you do know that is happening, or you should know, then you have a duty to get rid of it and prevent it from happening. And if you don't prevent it, then you're on the hook at the end of the day if somebody is trafficked at your institution,'" said Kent.

Civil lawsuits can also be a catalyst to ignite meaningful, across-the-board change in culture and society. Kent said settlements might demand non-monetary changes, like more training for hotel or truck stop employees on how to identify red flags, or better safety protocols put into place at a business.

Pinter said the goal of her organization, the National Center on Sexual Exploitation (NCOSE) Law Center, is to spur fundamental changes by targeting corporations rather than individuals. "We want to see change from the top down," she said. "We want those big actors who are actually making the big money from all of these traffickers, to go down. That's what we think is going to have the most lasting effect. It's such an opportunity to change society and to educate the public."

Pushing for change is not always easy, however, especially for trafficking survivors involved in lawsuits. "It's still litigation," Pinter said. "You're still going to face defendants, although [with NCOSE] it's more of an impersonal defendant, like a corporation, and not the trafficker." She said there will still be some "nasty lawyers who are going to put pressure on the victim." Kent agrees that civil cases can be highly unpleasant for trafficking survivors. "These cases are adversarial by nature. All lawsuits are. ... There are lawyers on the other side fighting this case," he said. The process can also be invasive for survivors, who are "claiming damages relative to trauma that they have experienced. The other side has an opportunity to challenge that," Kent said. He added that there is no guarantee of an outcome in civil or criminal cases.

Survivors who want to file a human trafficking lawsuit under the TVPRA should be aware of the statute of limitations, which is ten years after the survivor is separated from the trafficking situation. Or, if the trafficking happened when the survivor was a minor, the statute of limitations is ten years after the survivor turns eighteen. However, there are exceptions. For one thing, some states have anti-trafficking laws where the statute of limitations is different from the TVPRA. Also, there's the discovery rule, which points to when a survivor realizes that certain problems are related to her former trafficking, according to Kent. For example, a survivor might realize through therapy that her PTSD symptoms stem from being trafficked twenty years earlier. In that case, the statute of limitations would begin at the time of her realization, or discovery. However, not all courts interpret the discovery rule in the same way, so it might not apply the same way in every case.

Another consideration of criminal and civil cases is the level of involvement for the survivor. In the criminal justice system, the trafficking survivor is not necessarily part of the case, according to Kent. In a criminal case, the prosecution represents the state against the perpetrator, meaning "they don't necessarily represent the interest of the victim or survivor," said Kent. Thus, "the victim has very little control … because the state has an interest in protecting the public."

A civil case, on the other hand, "is the survivor's case," according to Pinter. "In criminal court, the prosecutor is working for the state. … But here in civil litigation, the survivor is the client. So, the attorney is working for the survivor. They're not working for anyone else. Even though the attorney will have their legal advice about what's the best avenue to take, at the end of the day, it's the survivor who calls the shots."

Each type of case has its advantages. In criminal prosecution, "the survivor can obtain a sense of justice because their perpetrators may be convicted and go to jail. They're off the streets, so this can't happen to another individual," Kent said. "The victim gets a chance to face their accuser in court and tell the story of what happened to them, and society is protected." On the other hand, an advantage of a civil case is that survivors do not have to take the stand and testify if they do not want to. Also, civil cases can bring larger societal changes.

Since civil and criminal cases are two separate entities, Kent points out, survivors can initiate a civil lawsuit even if a prosecutor or U.S. attorney declines to prosecute a case criminally. Sometimes, civil litigation can even open the door to criminal charges. "The ultimate goal of (civil) litigation is not to put someone in jail, although many times, this calls a lot of attention and evidence to law enforcement that ends up leading to a criminal investigation," said Pinter.

As we have seen, the TVPA, TVPRA and other federal laws have opened many doors for sex trafficking survivors to pursue justice against their traffickers. However, the law alone does not stop sex trafficking in the U.S. According to Gilmer, the law alone cannot stop sex trafficking. "As long as people have the resources and as long as people have the desire to purchase sex, and as long as there are people who are willing to exploit others, it's going to continue to happen," he said. "And some of those are issues we can't address legally. We can arrest our way out of a problem. We can arrest a person and put them in jail. We can't change their hearts. It's really a heart issue."

Their identity and who they are is not wrapped up in what they've done or what's been done to them.

PENNY BILLINGS

| six |

Getting Help

'I couldn't believe I actually spoke up'

Angela's story in her own words:

One day, my aunt—my dad's sister—was coming to pick me up for my sixth birthday. That day, because she was coming to pick me up, I don't know why but this thing in me rose up to tell my mother. Like, enough is enough, I'm telling my mother this guy [her mom's boyfriend] is touching us. I don't know why I did it to this day. I just said, "Mom this guy is touching us, and it's very uncomfortable, and I don't want to do that anymore." And my mother just kind of went pale and said nothing, just nothing at all. And the guy came around and, no wonder because she's scared of him, she just stayed quiet. But I remember that she finally approached him and said, "Hey my daughter's saying this." And he's like, "Oh no, I would never do that." But I said, "Look, it's written all over his face." Because I remember that his face turned really red, with veins all over. I couldn't believe I actually spoke up.

So, my aunt was coming to get us. My mom actually got us dressed. I think it was her way of saying, get out and be safe. And she let my aunt take us and put us in the car and everything. Never said a word. And then that night my aunt, giving my sister and me a shower, asked, "Has anybody ever touched you? Has anybody ever done anything?" And my sister finally broke down and shared the whole story.

At that point, my uncle was a police officer. We called him and he said there's a procedure we have to do. He immediately got us to the precinct. And they gave us these dolls with a penis and a vagina and, said, "Where? Show us what happened. Can you enact this?" It was very uncomfortable. It was just weird. But yeah, we did it. Then immediately they went to go get the guy, but I think at that point he knew, so he booked it. And my mom was nowhere to be found, either. So, they said, "We're going to put these kids in foster care because they need a place to stay, unless you're willing to keep them. Family foster." And my aunt was like, "I don't know." She loves us but she had a little apartment, and her own three kids.

And she had to ask my uncle and he was like, "absolutely," because he's the greatest man I've ever met. And he's like, "We've got to save them." But when she went to the church, the church was like, "Oh no, that's a really big responsibility. You don't know what you're getting yourself into. I don't think you should do that." And they kind of said it like it was from God. So, my aunt was like, "That just doesn't sound like God to me." And so, she said yes to keeping us until my mom got herself together or whatever. And we immediately stayed with her. She had to get all the things foster care wants you to—better beds and stuff.

My aunt was very strict sometimes. But she was very in command of her home and that was good. She taught us a lot of boundaries.

Angela lived with her aunt and uncle until she was 14. Then the courts made her and her sister move in with their father for a while, and then they went back to their mother. At seventeen, Angela became a victim of human sex trafficking. After a couple of years in that life, Angela was arrested. She stayed with her mother briefly, then went back to her boyfriend's. From there, her story continues below.

This is where God intervened. I started having dreams about the Lord coming back to the Earth. And then, my aunt invites me to a Christian concert. There's going to be a bunch of Christians there that I grew up with. I was like, "Uh, I don't know about that." I was supposed to go to this club. I didn't know if I could stay away from drugs and drinking. But something in me was like, "Go, go." So finally, I called her at the last minute and I said, "You know what, I'll go." But they had already left, so I ended up riding with my uncle, in the back with all the speakers and the equipment for the concert. But as soon as I get there, I just felt the love of God and all these beautiful people. So many familiar faces because I grew up for several years by then in the same church.

So, I'm seeing all these wonderful people who are grown up now and are preachers and leaders, and they're so welcoming. And I just felt dirty. All of a sudden, I felt dirty. If they only knew the things I had done, if they only knew the people I had been with, the marriages I might have destroyed, the type of people I've been involved with. They just wouldn't understand. Or they would treat me like a victim and that's something I never wanted.

So, I went to the concert. I had already said, I'm not going to do this life anymore. I'm going to fight this. I'm going to make sure I stay away from those areas. I went to bed that night hearing the voice of God in my heart.

It was exciting, but at the same time it was so heavy on my heart, like there's something happening around me and in me that I can't explain. It was so powerful. At the concert, I was going to the stalls to smoke some weed to calm down because I kept feeling this, hearing a voice in me. I stayed with my aunt that night because it was late. And I was planning to go back to my boyfriend the next day, who I was still sort of living with back and forth, even though he was very abusive.

That night when I went to sleep in her house, I had another dream. In the dream, I was in a club. And I was dancing and I was having fun. And it was the same old, same old. The dark room with the lights and the party and the drugs and the drinking. And then, I see my aunt in the club, who raised me, who was the most influential Christian in my life. And then my Sunday school teacher, who also was always the best teacher. So, this was like God showing me two people that he had used constantly to build me up in my life. And they resembled everything that he wanted from me. And I had a choice in the dream. I could go with them or I could stay in that situation in the middle of the club doing the same old thing over and over. You would think the dream would end like that. But there was a back room in the club and the room was empty except for some crates. And they both took me by the arm, and we locked our arms together. And then just waited. And all of a sudden, there was just a joy and a presence and light that just flowed over us. And it was so beautiful. It was so peaceful there.

That's when I felt for the first time that I belong to God. I woke up immediately. I didn't have any clothes that were appropriate. I wore miniskirts and weird clothes that made me feel slutty, because my aunt had raised me to be very modest. But I didn't care. I put on my clothes and I ran to church, which was the church I grew up in. I ran to it because it was Sunday morning and my aunt does worship and leads there. She and my uncle are elders. I ran into the church. I sat in the back and I just remember what my Sunday school teacher said. So, I prayed and gave my heart to the Lord. When I left, I told my cousin about it. My cousin told my aunt, because they had always been really concerned for me because they knew I was very independent and strong-willed and they knew I was probably in some bad situation that nobody could reach me from. I went back home to my boyfriend and he was sitting on the couch smoking weed and drinking. And I felt in my heart, I'm done with that. I want to live a different life. So, I told him that and he's like, "You're such a slut," and he just started flipping on me.

I thought, I just have to get through this night. I'm going to go to sleep and I'm just leaving. I knew I shouldn't have even gone there. I was going to sleep that night and my boyfriend was drunk and he tried to rape me. He'd never really done that. He was being evil with me, flipping. And so, I just prayed, "Lord, help me with this situation. I don't want to do anything with him. I don't want to have sex anymore. I'm tired of giving my body, my life, my everything to people just because they want it. I want to be in control." And as soon as I prayed that, he immediately knocked out, passed out asleep. But he had his hand on me, holding me down so I couldn't get up or go anywhere. He was very controlling and possessive. I stayed awake all night, but I laid there. When the morning came, I pretended like everything was okay. And when he left the house, I packed all my clothes and I took what I could.

At this time, I had just gotten my first job. An actual real job, and I was so proud of myself. I felt really proud of that. I was a receptionist making $6.50 an hour, so to me this was like nothing! After making the money I was making with the massages and escorting, it was poverty to me. But it was work. And I really wanted to work and make money legally. I wanted to know what that felt like. And so, I got this job. I was eighteen now. I took my job super serious and did everything the best I could. I had only been working there three days when I gave my heart to the Lord. So, my aunt called me at work. She wanted to be back in my life at this point, helping to guide my life. This goes back to my rule problem. I allow myself to be controlled in other ways but I didn't want to be controlled in the right way. Don't tell me to do good things. Don't make me do this. And my aunt said, "Listen, you have not allowed yourself to be a teenager. I don't know what you've been doing but it's definitely like you acted like you're an adult. You need to go back to being a teenager. Following rules, learning order and being taken care of a little bit. Let us help you. And so, we want you to come live with us." At sixteen, she had asked me to live with her and I did, and I would never come home some nights. I just couldn't be responsible or follow her rules, so she kicked me out. For her to invite me back was very redemptive.

I was like, "I don't know about that." But then I knew from the night before I had to get out of my ex-boyfriend's house. And so, my uncle picked me up after work. And the next day, they took me back to the house when my ex-boyfriend was at work to get my clothes and everything. And I was looking out the car window thinking, "Wow, I'll never see this guy again." And I did it. From then on, I lived with them. I shared with them some of my story, but not everything because it just really broke their hearts. They couldn't even hear some of the things I was doing. They just could not believe I was up at midnight or one in the morning in strangers' houses or hotel rooms, tipsy, just doing things like this. They couldn't handle it. They were like, "You could have been killed, you could have been beaten."

Chapter 4 explains that Angela went to college, eventually earning her master's degree at a seminary. She later got help for her trauma and PTSD. Today, she is married with three children. I asked Angela what she would say to other people who are sex trafficking victims or survivors, especially if they want to get out or if they do not believe they're being victimized.

Very good question. Well, I always will say the verse Jeramiah 29:11 to them first: "God knows the plans he has for you and they are for good and not for evil. To prosper you and give you a future." I'd like to help them know that these people [traffickers and buyers] don't have a future for them that's good. Some of the people I met were people in the church, caliber people in positions of politics. People who look good on the screen, people who look good in person, like the Hasidic Jew of all people, with the curls and big outfits. He's a rabbi and he's coming in for his hand job. You start to think that everyone is really just like this, so what's the point of leaving this to go to another situation like that.

I would tell them that that's just not true. There are plenty of good people who don't think like that, that they are actually good in their core and there's always hope.

I would always tell them if they have one family member who prays and loves them, to make sure they stay in contact with them no matter what. That's very important because without my aunt, I'll be honest with you, I probably would have reversed right back into the situation. It would have just kept going.

So, that's what I would tell them. Jeremiah 29:11. I mean, I don't know how I'm here today with three beautiful kids. I just feel so blessed to be able to take care of this next generation. I'm always talking about abuse with them. I have to. I have to let my daughter know I was abused. We're very particular about people and what the kids are doing.

I asked Angela how else her trafficking experience and recovery has shaped her as a mother.

It made me really tough, but I also realize I can't overdo it. Sometimes I'm too hypervigilant with well-meaning people because I am just so scared of that happening to my daughter or to my sons and then I find out later. It would just kill me inside. So, there's also that fear that keeps going. I believe that's a part of PTSD, thinking even friends or neighbors could be someone that does this to your kid. And so, it's hard to think purely about everyone. I tend to think toward the worst situation. I realize not everybody lives like that, because when you haven't been exposed to that kind of abuse, you're not thinking like that. I would have loved to be a little bit more like those people, but that's just not who I am.

* * *

HELPING SURVIVORS LEAVE

At several key moments in her life, Angela reached out for help. She told her mother when she was six that she was being sexually abused. Then at age eighteen, she told her aunt and uncle about being trafficked and allowed them to help her. These were hard decisions that changed the trajectory of Angela's life.

Some advocates make a distinction between *helping* a trafficking victim and *rescuing* her. Amy Wagar, an advocate for Worthy[2] (Worthy Squared) and a trainer for the Child Trafficking Solutions Project, said she steers away from saying her organization rescues survivors because in the long run, survivors rescue themselves.

They are the ones who do the hard work of transitioning into a new life.

"They have made the decision to come out of this life and to seek help. And they are trying to reclaim their life, their decisions, their choices, their future," said Wagar. "When they make the decision to go to a facility or to get help, that's their decision. We're just transporting them, so that they can reclaim what's theirs."[36]

Shelia Simpkins-McClain, MSSW,[37] Director of Education and Outreach at Thistle Farms in Nashville, Tennessee, agrees with Wagar. "You are the hero of your story when you survived all of that. This is not an easy road when you get into the survivor side of the trauma. There's so much work that you have to do," said Simpkins-McClain, who is a sex trafficking survivor. "When we say survivor, I'm talking about truly being a survivor. It's hard work." She added that she wants to empower survivors to dream instead of dreaming for them. "I am a resource now for the women who are in the program, to walk with them. Not carry them. When you carry, you become an enabler."

Empowering victims and survivors is crucial. One of the most effective ways is to use a trauma-informed approach, which includes enabling people to make their own choices, treating them with dignity, and establishing trust. First, victims must decide whether or not to leave the life and whether to get help. As Wagar explains, many victims who are still in the life do not realize they are victims and that crimes are being committed against them. In those cases, responsible organizations do not try to force the victims to leave their traffickers. Trafficking Hope's approach is to make friends with women working as prostitutes or in strip clubs; bring them food, hygiene items, flowers and other gifts; and let them know that help is available if they want a different way of life. After that, it is up to the women to choose. The organization does not pressure or manipulate the women, but gives them the dignity of making their own decisions.

Glen Buckley's organization, 731 Rescue, has the same approach. Buckley and his team did a recent undercover operation in Nashville where they used a website to set up "dates" with prostitutes, many of whom were being trafficked. When the women showed up at the hotel room, and when the pimp was nowhere in sight, anti-trafficking advocates came into the room and gave the women a choice. They could leave right then and go to the Scarlet Rope Project safehouse that Buckley helped start, or they could go back to their pimp. "The girls would get to choose whether they wanted to leave with us or just walk out the door and continue what they're doing," said Buckley. "If they decided to leave, and if the deal that we set up online was two hundred bucks, we gave them the two hundred bucks so they wouldn't get beat up."

Buckley's organization, however, learned that approach the hard way. When he first opened the safehouse, the rescue team set up their undercover operations, pulled the women from hotels without asking if they wanted to go, then took them straight to the safehouse. "And what we found was, in a day or two, or a week or two, they're running away from the safehouse," said Buckley. "We were racking our brains trying to figure out why this was happening."

The team finally realized how much the women feared their traffickers. "They've convinced her that if she tries to leave, they'll kill her and they'll kill her kids," said Buckley. The women also ran away from the shelter because their traffickers were their sole source of everything. "Whether it be shelter, whether it be food, whether it be her source of narcotics—with a lot of traffickers, their hook to hold onto you is narcotics," said Buckley. "And so, if he's your only source, you can't leave your source."

Buckley's team at first didn't take the time to build trust with the women they were trying to help. When that method didn't work, the team tried a different way, where the women could choose to stay in the safehouse for a few days to rest and eat before being turned over to law enforcement to face charges pending against them. While they were in jail, Buckley said, the women would detox and catch up on their sleep. "They had time to think," he said. When the women went back to court, advocates from the Scarlet Rope Project met them there. The judge and prosecutor in that jurisdiction agreed to give the women a choice. They could go through the Scarlet Rope Project restoration program and get all of their charges dropped upon completion of the program. If they didn't finish the program, they would go to jail for six months (the maximum time for a prostitution conviction, according to Buckley). "We didn't force them to be there. If they wanted to get up and walk out the door, they got up and walked out the door. But they had this incentive to stay," he said. When his team implemented that strategy, the safehouse's recidivism rate went down and the success rate went up, meaning more women completed the program.

The WellHouse, a residential program for women who have been sex trafficked, also takes the approach of giving women the freedom to make choices. "I'm more hopeful than I have ever been that people can change if given the opportunity. But it's completely up to them," said Carolyn Potter, CEO of The WellHouse. "You cannot force change on anyone. I don't feel like I have to rescue and force anyone to change. I feel like it's my job to offer that opportunity and the grace to help them through it."

Creating an atmosphere of respect and trust with survivors is key. Real Escape from the Sex Trade (REST) of Seattle, Washington, strongly emphasizes treating clients, including their LGBTQ+ clients, with respect. Audrey Baedke, REST Cofounder and Programs Manager, notes that some staff members at REST believe that homosexuality is a sin. "It's important for us at REST to allow everyone to have their beliefs, and to accept those beliefs and be respectful of them," Baedke said. However, she added, staff members who are against homosexuality must not let their views prevent clients from receiving proper services. "It's really important to recognize that regardless of your personal beliefs, the beliefs that should be unifying us is the recognition that every human has dignity and worth. And because of that, they should be treated with that respect," she said.

Earning trust takes time, as Oasis Consulting Group Founder Sill Davis points out. "Don't expect them to just come in and lay out their whole lives before you. You have to earn that respect and trust," said Davis. "And that can take days, months, sometimes years depending on how long you've worked with the client."

Penny Billings, a volunteer at The WellHouse, is taking just that approach. "I don't know their stories. And I respect them and love them too much to ask them, even a year later," Billings said. "I don't push. Even the girl that I mentor, I don't push her. She opens up from time to time and I may ask her a question here and there. But I am still trying to gain her trust."

Survivors need time to heal without being pushed. Sex trafficking survivors do not just "move on" from the trauma of being trafficked. Angela has been away from trafficking for more than twenty years and she still deals with PTSD and anxiety. Her interview for this book is the first time she has talked about her trafficking experience nearly in its entirety. It took two decades for her to be ready. "It is very private and there's also an element of shame attached to it, even though a lot of it is not necessarily my fault," she said.

Simpkins-McClain argues that, like Angela, all survivors need plenty of time to heal, especially before they try to help others. Some anti-trafficking groups seek out survivor-leaders as a way to give their organizations more credibility. "Having a survivor on the team means you can say that you are survivor-led and survivor-informed, which is pretty important in the anti-trafficking alliance," said Simpkins-McClain. But she said it is better for survivors to heal significantly and be qualified before taking on a leadership role. "Just because you're a survivor, does not make you a survivor-leader. It is not your responsibility to educate anti-trafficking organizations on the work that they're doing."

Simpkins-McClain learned this for herself when she took on a leadership role that she soon realized she was not ready for. "I did a pretty good job, don't get me wrong," she said. She helped the organization open a couple of safehouses and did some other progressive work. "But at the end of the day, I was not qualified for that position. And I truly felt like I was doing harm to the women that I was serving." Simpkins-McClain said she did not yet have leadership skills and did not listen to others. "I thought I knew everything. And I just stopped listening. Because I was the survivor. I know what works for us." Her only qualifications were her own personal trafficking experience and the knowledge of what had worked for her. She quickly learned that what worked for her does not necessarily work for others. She resigned and went back to her previous job so she could go to college and "become employable again."

Hiring unqualified survivors can harm not only the organization, but also the survivors themselves, said Simpkins-McClain. "I got that position because I was a survivor, not because I was qualified for the position," she said. "In a sense, it's almost like re-exploiting all over again."

EFFECT ON WORKERS

Helping sex trafficking victims and survivors can leave its mark on those who do the work. Whether they are volunteers, leaders, counselors, law enforcement, attorneys or anyone else whose lives are touched by sex trafficking, few walk away unchanged.

"All of it has been very eye-opening," said Billings. After volunteering at The WellHouse for a year, Billings has an entirely different perspective on human sex trafficking. "I think I'm more surprised that there could be somebody so evil, so cruel, that would treat another human being like this. When I hear the stories that the traffickers are sometimes family members, that blows me away even more."

Billings was nervous about volunteering at first because she had never met a sex trafficking victim. In the past, she had led small groups for what she calls "church ladies," but never for a group of women with deep trauma. "I didn't know what to expect from these women. It really kind of scared me," she said. It didn't take long for her to realize what she was getting into. "The minute I stepped into that house, my heart melted," she said. "Those ladies just stole my heart. I've been hooked ever since. They're absolutely beautiful women, every one of them."

Billings knows one woman who left the program and went back to her trafficker. "It broke my heart," she said. "But it's not for me to understand, or to expect them to just change overnight. It doesn't happen like that."

Working with trafficking victims has changed Billings' life by clarifying her personal goals. She went to school full-time to get a Christian ministry certificate and said she now knows she is meant to help and lead women. She has also learned a new approach for working with others. "You have to go into it with an open heart and an open mind and an open agenda," she said. In addition, Billings is a pageant contestant who chose human sex trafficking as her platform. In her role as Ms. Classic Continental 2021, Billings reached a national audience with her platform.

Potter, CEO of The WellHouse, has also learned a great deal from working with sex trafficking survivors. On the negative side, Potter found that people can be far more treacherous than she realized. "I do know the world is a worse place than I knew it to be beforehand. People will do things that I would never have thought before," she said. On the other hand, Potter's experience with trafficking survivors has increased her Christian faith. "I was a believer beforehand—believing God and trusting God," she said. "But now it is a way of life. It is literal. I completely depend on the spiritual part of it to get me through." Potter said her experience has also helped her set better boundaries, from taking time off work to dealing with clients who learned to survive by manipulating others. Like Billings, Potter said she falls in love with the women who come through the program.

However, anti-sex-trafficking work is not always a heartwarming story. Working with sex trafficking survivors is not for everyone. Potter had an employee who was smart and talented, but resigned soon after she was hired. "We all loved her. But it just didn't mesh," said Potter. "She just could not deal with the everyday life of this work. You have to be flexible and be able to roll with it. And not everybody can do that."

Anti-sex-trafficking work is filled with triumph and purpose, but also heartache. Practically everyone who works with sex trafficking survivors has heart-wrenching stories of those who refused to believe the modeling agency was a trick, or who left a recovery program to return to her trafficker, or who went missing never to be heard from again, or who could not see her own worth as a human being. They tell stories of women and children being beaten, raped, drugged and killed. Human sex trafficking is a violent world, and those who work with trafficking victims and survivors must be able to handle it. They have to handle the trauma and survival responses of survivors, which are not always pretty. Sex trafficking victims sometimes learn to manipulate and lie so they can live another day. They can carry those behaviors with them into recovery programs. "Just because we're survivors doesn't mean that we leave all of our

survival tools at the door whenever we come in [to a program],"
said Simpkins-McClain.

Teresa Collier said some trafficking survivors are street-smart
and savvy. "They have to be, in order to survive in the type of environment that they're living in," said Collier, a Forensic Child Interview Specialist, a trainer for the Child Trafficking Solutions Project,
and former Intelligence Analyst for the Alabama Law Enforcement
Agency. Collier also interviews adult sex trafficking victims and
survivors. "They're not exactly that meek and mild innocent survivor that a lot of people think that they might be," she said. When
Collier interviews trafficking survivors, she encounters hostility,
deception, exaggerations and downplaying of what happened.

Wagar sees the same reactions when she talks to victims on the
street. "While we may have a great heart about it and we want to
see them set free and help them, they may initially be combative,
or put off, or scared of you, or concerned about talking to you," she
said.[38] As Wagar described in Chapter 4, trafficking victims have
spit, cursed and screamed at her. She has seen a pimp beat up a
woman. She has likely seen many other hard things that she doesn't
talk about. And still, she loves her work. "If you're called to something, you live your life on purpose for it," she said.

Douglas Gilmer, who helps train sex-trafficking advocates, explains to trainees that victims often react from their trauma. "You're
going to hear things and see things that are probably going to
really disturb you, but you can't react to it," said Gilmer, a federal
law enforcement agent in Birmingham, Alabama, who works with
human trafficking victims. "You just have to sit there. You just have
to accept it," Gilmer said. "Remember what your role is. At that
moment, you're there for the victims."[39]

Trafficking advocates' efforts reach far beyond the victims and
survivors. Gilmer has seen law enforcement officers and survivors'
families benefit from the work of advocates. This happens, he said,

when advocates stay true to their role and keep the right attitude. "If they came in with a very legalistic mindset, or if evangelism or proselytization was their number one priority, I guarantee that would be a turnoff," said Gilmer. He said the advocates he works with conduct themselves professionally. "They're there to do what it is they've been called to do. They stay in their lane," he said. "They work their mission. That helps break down some of those barriers."[40]

Elisha McNeal points out how hard, but rewarding, working with trafficking victims can be. She quotes one of her program's employees: "This is the best worst job I've ever had." McNeal, BSW,[41] Director of Community Engagement and Training at Gracehaven in Columbus, Ohio, explains that employees must give clients a safe space to heal, the best care possible, and hope. It's difficult, she said, because Gracehaven works with youth who have experienced some of the worst possible trauma. "Those things are hard," said McNeal. "But also, it's the best job, because they let us walk this journey with them. And we get glimpses of them experiencing freedom and love and letting their walls down. And there's just nothing like that."

Simpkins-McClain is an advocate who has experienced trafficking personally. "My passion is to be a part of the individuals' healing process. Just a little piece of it. It does something for me to be able to watch a survivor coming in in that cocoon and then blossom into this really, really beautiful butterfly," she said. "You get to watch them fly away and just live really beautiful lives. It's so rewarding on so many different levels."

HEALING AND HOPE

Healing from sex-trafficking-related trauma and PTSD is not easy, but there is hope.

"It takes a great amount of courage, grit and perseverance. And a willingness to engage in therapy for a period of time," said Connie Oden, LICSW,[42] of Birmingham, Alabama. "With treatment, it is possible to make significant recovery. Many people do. People who actually follow through with treatment do very well."

Therapy is important because it helps people understand their patterns and change patterns that no longer work, Oden said. "If you have not developed the insight about the dance of abuse and what constitutes abuse, you're not going to see any other way," she added. "A lot of times, people are motivated by simply believing that's the only way they can survive."

For people who have deep trauma from childhood sexual abuse, which is a common precursor to being trafficked, intense therapy is even more important. "Childhood sexual abuse victims really have to do a lot more work. They need concentrated treatment," said Oden. But even people with lifelong sexual trauma can heal. "If they can find a good therapist, some of that will begin to turn around," Oden said. "There's the opportunity to begin to see the other side of recovery. And recovery really does work."

Simpkins-McClain knows recovery works because she is a thriving example. She recalls her personal transition from sex trafficking victim to survivor. The switch happened when she entered a program safehouse. "Right when I took a step into that house, I became a survivor because I was no longer being victimized," she said, adding that every survivor has her own transition depending on her healing process.

Another trafficking survivor who helps other survivors build new lives is Rachel Thomas, M. Ed.,[43] of Houston, Texas, director of Sowers Education Group and the lead author of *Ending the Game: An Intervention Curriculum for Survivors of Sex Trafficking*. The curriculum helps survivors "increase hope for a future outside of the life," said Thomas. "That this is not the only way that I can pay my bills. This is not all I'm good for. I'm not damaged goods." The curriculum teaches survivors they are loveable and they are "still all the things [they were] created to be."

Potter has many success stories of graduates from The Well-House. "There are quite a few actually that stand out for me," said Potter. "We've got several who have regained custody of their own children. They are just fabulous and are doing a great job." One WellHouse graduate got her commercial driver license (CDL) and became a truck driver. Others went to college, some making the Dean's List and earning other honors.

Dr. Carolyn West, Professor of Clinical Psychology at the University of Washington in Tacoma, Washington, is another advocate who sees a bright future for survivors who do the work to heal. West works with programs that use the arts to help survivors "create images of themselves that are more positive." She has found success by helping Black girls and women find healthier images of themselves than what they see in certain music videos, for example. She said some videos "show such a narrow definition of who and what Black girls are and can be." The programs she's involved with provide respected role models and mentors who teach girls and women that they have options other than sex trafficking.

To Collier, success can mean helping a trafficking victim get out of her dangerous situation. Collier enjoys her role as a forensic interviewer because it often leads to positive results when a victim or survivor is honest with her. "Hopefully somebody will be arrested, or the victim will get the services they need," said Collier. Even when perpetrators do not get arrested, Collier's interviews sometimes result in survivors getting placed at a recovery facility "where they have a real chance of getting out of that situation. To me, that's as much of a success as anything. Giving somebody the resources to get out of that life, because it's a horrible life."

Gilmer wants trafficking victims and survivors to know from a law enforcement perspective that help is available. "We're committed to helping them. We're committed to getting them out of that lifestyle, and holding those responsible, accountable," said Gilmer. He added that trafficking victims and survivors are not the criminals. "They are not the ones that need to worry about being in trouble. We've got the tools and the resources available to help them. And I want them to know that they're not forgotten."

Anti-trafficking efforts benefit entire communities and not just individuals. Kathy Wilson, Cofounder of the Cullman County (Alabama) Human Trafficking Task Force, said no human sex trafficking cases were tried in Cullman County before the task force existed. At the time of her interview in 2020, three human trafficking cases were pending in the county.

On a statewide level, the number of human sex trafficking cases in Alabama has continued to increase since 2010, when the state passed anti-trafficking legislation. Also, more than five-hundred patrol officers and state troopers in Alabama have been trained through the Interdiction for the Protection of Children (IPC) program, according to Collier. IPC training teaches law enforcement to identify children who are missing or being exploited or trafficked, and to identify people who are a high-risk threat to children, such as sex offenders, Collier said. She added that law enforcement has conducted more than thirty IPC stops in the state since the training began in 2017, resulting in child pornography being uncovered, suspects arrested and children recovered from offenders. "We never had anything like that before we started doing the training," said Collier.

Hope exists for human sex trafficking survivors and for the communities we all live in. The work is hard on victims and survivors, on anti-trafficking advocates, and on everyone else who cares about human sex trafficking victims and survivors. The good news is, plenty of people are doing the hard work anyway. Tell everyone around you that human sex trafficking is happening in your community through smartphones and gaming systems. It is happening in your community behind closed doors where adults sell their kids for drugs, alcohol, cash or anything else they can trade them for. Sex trafficking is happening in ritzy neighborhoods and in low-income neighborhoods. But anti-sex-trafficking work is also happening, and you have become a part of it by educating yourself.

| seven |

Resources

If you are being forced to perform sex acts against your wishes, or if you know of someone who is, get help here:

In an emergency, call 911 first. Then use the options below.

Polaris Project National Human Trafficking Hotline
Call: 1 (888) 373-7888
Text: 233733 (Be Free)
Online: polarisproject.org (Live Chat)

U.S. Homeland Security Investigations Tip Line
Call: 1 (866) 347-2423

National Center for Missing and Exploited Children
Online: report.cybertip.org

WEBSITES

Alabama Human Trafficking Task Force

www.enditalabama.org

Alicia Kozak

www.aliciakozak.com

Alicia Project

www.aliciaproject.org

Alliance to End Slavery and Trafficking

www.endslaverynow.org

Blue Campaign, Department of Homeland Security

ww.dhs.gov/blue-campaign

Common Sense Media

www.commonsensemedia.org (to research apps)

Demand Abolition

www.demandabolition.org

End It

www.enditmovement.com

Fight The New Drug

www.fightthenewdrug.org (info about pornography)

National Center for Missing and Exploited Children

www.connect.missingkids.org

Polaris

www.polarisproject.org

Shared Hope International

www.sharedhope.org/internetsafety (to research apps)

U.S. Congress

www.congress.gov (to read the TVPA and FOSTA-SESTA)

BOOKS

Some of these works are cited in this book and others were recommended by people I interviewed.

The Body Keeps the Score: Brain, Mind, and Body in the Healing of Trauma by Bessel van der Kolk, M.D. (Penguin Publishing Group, 2018)

Braving the Wilderness: The Quest for True Belonging and the Courage to Stand Alone by Brené Brown, Ph.D. (Random House Trade Paperbacks, 2019)

Breath, New Science of a Lost Art by James Nestor (Riverhead Books, 2020)

Ending the Game: An Intervention Curriculum for Survivors of Human Sex Trafficking by Rachel Thomas (Journal of Women and Criminal Justice, 2021)

Girls Like Us: Fighting for a World Where Girls are Not for Sale, an Activist Finds Her Calling and Heals Herself by Rachel Lloyd (Harper, 2011)

Human Trafficking: A Comprehensive Exploration of Modern Day Slavery by Wendy Stickle, Shelby Hickman and Christine White (Sage Publications, Inc., 2019)

Human Trafficking 101: Stories, Stats, and Solutions by Amy Joy (Amy Joy, 2018)

Trauma and Recovery: The Aftermath of Violence—From Domestic Abuse to Political Terror by Judith Herman, M.D. (Basic Books, 1992)

PAPERS AND REPORTS

The Last Frontier was recommended by people I interviewed and the other reports were cited in this book.

The Last Frontier: Practice Guidelines for the Treatment of Complex Trauma and Trauma Informed Care and Service Delivery by Dr. Cathy Kezelman and Dr. Pam Stavropoulos

Trafficking in Persons Report by the U.S. Department of State

Who Buys Sex? Understanding and Disrupting Illicit Market Demand by Demand Abolition

ORGANIZATIONS

The organizations below are only a few of the anti-trafficking organizations that exist. The descriptions about the organizations are taken from their own websites. For anyone wanting to help in the fight against human sex trafficking, many of these organizations accept donations to help continue their work.

731 Rescue
[www.facebook.com/731rescue]

"At 731 Rescue we are passionate about giving back to our community and one of the ways we give back is by participating in the fight against Human Trafficking."

Center for Innovation in Health Policy and Practice
[www.nasmhpd.org/content/national-center-trauma-informed-care-nctic-0]

"NASMHPD's (National Association of State Mental Health Program Directors) Center for Innovation in Health Policy and Practice promotes trauma-informed practices in the delivery of services to people who have experienced violence and trauma and are seeking support for recovery and healing."

Child Trafficking Solutions Project
[www.facebook.com/childtraffickingsolutionsproject]

"The Child Trafficking Solutions Project is a broad-based coalition of law enforcement, juvenile justice, NGO's, healthcare providers, and child protective service agencies that seeks to rescue and restore child victims of sex trafficking."

Cullman County Human Trafficking Task Force
[www.facebook.com/cullman-county-human-trafficking-task-force-870585096352748]

"Cullman County Human Trafficking Task Force: creating awareness, educating our community and actively participating to bring an end to human trafficking."

Ending the Game
[www.endingthegame.com]

"Ending The Game© (ETG) is the nation's leading 'coercion resiliency' curriculum in the field of human trafficking. This psychoeducational curriculum empowers survivors by providing a framework to understand and uproot harmful psychological coercion (a.k.a. 'The Game') that many victims have been subjected to during or before their exploitation experience."

GenerateHope
[www.generatehope.org]

"GenerateHope is a safe place for survivors of sex trafficking to heal and find restoration in long-term housing and trauma-informed therapy, education, and vocational support. Since recovery from sexual exploitation is a long-term process, GenerateHope provides safety, community and individualized life skills support to work through the deep trauma and discover a healthy, purpose-filled life."

Gracehaven
[www.gracehaven.me]

"Gracehaven is a faith-based, 501C3 non-profit organization. We serve any minor under 18 who has been sexually exploited without regard to race, color, religion, gender, national origin, disability, or sexual orientation. We provide care for sexually exploited children by providing comprehensive, client-centered services."

Grace to Glory Counseling
[www.gracetoglorycounseling.org]

Dr. Michelle Harrison "specializes in addressing trauma, addictions, and aiding women who have been trafficked and in recovery through her non-profit private practice."

Human Trafficking Prevention Project, University of Maryland School of Law
[www.mvlslaw.org/ht]

"The Human Trafficking Prevention Project (HTPP), a partnership between Maryland Volunteer Lawyers Service and University of Baltimore School of Law, focuses on reducing the collateral consequences of criminal legal involvement for survivors of human trafficking and those populations made most vulnerable to exploitation."

National Center on Sexual Exploitation
[www.endsexualexploitation.org]

"We believe in a world free from sexual abuse and exploitation. We believe every human being deserves the opportunity to live life to its fullest potential; to pursue dreams and ambitions; express creativity and hone talents; seek beauty, truth, and faith; experience hope, joy, and love with family and friends—to thrive. Such a vision requires not only individuals and institutions that work towards its realization but also a culture that embraces its responsibility to preserve and protect human flourishing."

National Trafficking Sheltered Alliance
[www.shelteredalliance.org]

"A community of service providers for survivors of human trafficking."

Rescue 1 Global
[www.rescue1global.org]

"Rescue 1 Global is now an independent, full-scale prevention, rescue, and restoration mission" to fight sex trafficking.

REST (Real Escape from the Sex Trade)
[www.iwantrest.com]

"REST offers pathways to freedom, safety, and hope to individuals who have experienced the sex trade. Everyone deserves to be loved. Everyone deserves a life free from exploitation."

Scarlet Rope Project
[www.scarletropeproject.com]

"Working to prevent exploitation and provide escape from the bondage of sex trafficking."

Thistle Farms
[www.thistlefarms.org]

"The work of love is to keep lighting the way for millions of women still searching for a way out. For over 20 years, Thistle Farms has lit a pathway of healing and hope for women survivors of trafficking, prostitution, and addiction."

Trafficking Hope
[www.traffickinghope.org]

"We are hopeful activists fighting a global problem, one local solution at a time."

The WellHouse
[www.the-wellhouse.org]

"The WellHouse is a safe haven for female victims of human trafficking. We provide opportunities for restoration to female victims of human trafficking who have been sexually exploited through our emergency-, short-, and long-care programs. Our mission is simple: restore."

West Alabama Human Trafficking Task Force
[www.westalabamahttf.com]

"Our task force consists of officers from the Tuscaloosa Police Department, Northport Police Department, University of Alabama Police Department and Tuscaloosa County Sheriff's Office. We strive every day to educate and protect the citizens of Tuscaloosa County and the surrounding areas."

Worthy² (Worthy Squared)
[www.worthy2.org]

"Worthy² advocates for those who have been exploited through sex trafficking or commercial sex, so they may reclaim their dignity and self-worth."

ACKNOWLEDGEMENTS

First of all, thank you to Angela for telling your sex trafficking survival story with bravery and sincerity. You want your life story to help other people. It already has and it will help countless more.

Thank you to the people I interviewed for this book. You were generous with your time and knowledge. Your expertise is priceless and the work you do is invaluable. This book never would have happened without you.

Thank you to Amy Joy, author of *Human Trafficking 101: Stories, Stats, and Solutions* for your encouragement and advice.

Thank you to my writing group—Margaret Marston, Lori Cormier and Lucy Jaffe—for providing encouragement and feedback and for helping me believe in myself.

Thank you to my Mom, sisters and all of my family and friends who believed in me and in this book.

Thank you to friends and attorneys Jon and Jackie Wesson for writing the interview consent form and for letting me use your cabin in the woods for mental health breaks.

Thank you to Kylee Bunt for helping me transcribe hours and hours of interviews.

Thank you to Julie McLendon and Shannon West for educating me about anti-trafficking websites and for your enthusiasm for this book.

Thank you to Cheryl Mangum for offering your expertise on anatomy and physiology and for making sure I got all the details correct about the physiological effects of trauma.

Thank you to Lucy Jaffe, Danielle Cater and Kevin Beasley for reading and editing the manuscript. You caught typos and errors, asked all the right questions and made outstanding suggestions.

Thank you most of all to Jennifer Anders, my first reader and my number-one supporter in writing and in everything else. Your multiple readings of the manuscript and your thoughtful suggestions made it a better book. Without your support and encouragement, this book would not exist.

All of you who edited the book made it so much better than it could have ever been otherwise. Any remaining errors or omissions are mine.

NOTES

[1] To reach the Polaris National Human Trafficking Hotline, call 1 (888) 373-7888, text 233733 (Be Free), or chat with a live person at www.polarisproject.org.

[2] *Human Trafficking: A Comprehensive Exploration of Modern Day Slavery* by Wendy Stickle, Shelby Hickman and Christine White explores these lesser-discussed forms of human trafficking in detail. Their book is also an excellent resource for sex and labor trafficking information.

[3] For this book, Douglas Gilmer was not authorized to disclose which federal law enforcement agency he works for.

[4] Kathy Wilson is also a Juvenile Probation Officer, where she has worked with suspected sex trafficking victims.

[5] I first met and interviewed Amy Wagar when she was Alabama Director of Trafficking Hope. She stepped down from that position but is still heavily involved in anti-sex-trafficking work and training through the organizations she currently works with.

[6] Amy Joy, BSW MPA (Bachelor of Social Work and Master of Public Administration), is the Founder and Executive Director of Restoration Place, a faith-based nonprofit organization to help minor victims of sexual exploitation. She is also a national speaker on how to identify and respond to human trafficking. (This information is quoted from the back of her book, *Human Trafficking 101*.) I met Amy when she spoke at a sex trafficking training event in Cullman, Alabama.

[7] LICSW is Licensed Independent Clinical Social Worker. Oden is also a Registered Nurse.

[8] M. Ed. is Master of Education.

[9] People with opioid addictions are often treated with methadone, which mimics the effects of opioids.

[10] Scarlet Rope Project is a faith-based nonprofit organization that provides a place of healing for female sex trafficking survivors. Buckley is also former law enforcement in Western Tennessee.

[11] Investigators eventually discovered the IP address (Internet Protocol is a unique string of numbers that identifies computers that are used to access the Internet) of the man who terrorized the college student. The man was charged with digital exploitation.

[12] The dark web allows websites and users to operate on the Internet anonymously. Sites and users on the dark web are said to be untraceable. It reportedly has some legal websites, but is known for facilitating illegal activity.

[13] This is information Teresa Collier gave at the National Trafficking Sheltered Alliance anti-trafficking conference in September 2020. All other references to Collier are from a personal interview and emails unless otherwise noted.

[14] M. Ed. is Master of Education.

[15] LCSW is Licensed Clinical Social worker.

[16] LICSW is Licensed Independent Clinical Social Worker. Oden is also a Registered Nurse.

[17] LISW-S is Licensed Independent Social Worker with Supervision. C-DBT means Certified in Dialectical Behavior Therapy.

[18] Stockholm Syndrome occurs when a victim of trafficking, abduction or other abuse develops a psychological and emotional bond with the perpetrator.

[19] A "bottom" is usually one of a trafficker's long-time victims that he promotes to an authority position as a sort of manager over his other victims. Part of her job is to keep the other girls in line and to train them. Being a bottom does not mean she has an easier life. Sometimes the trafficker will savagely beat the bottom in front of his other victims to discourage them from misbehaving.

[20] This is information Teresa Collier gave at the National Trafficking Sheltered Alliance anti-trafficking conference in September 2020. All other references to Collier are from a personal interview and emails unless otherwise noted.

[21] M. Ed. is Master of Education.

[22] MSSW is Master of Science in Social Work.

[23] LCSW is Licensed Clinical Social Worker.

[24] From the National Trafficking Sheltered Alliance conference.

[25] From the National Trafficking Sheltered Alliance conference.

[26] From the National Trafficking Sheltered Alliance conference.

[27] From the National Trafficking Sheltered Alliance conference.

[28] From the National Trafficking Sheltered Alliance conference.

[29] "Girl on the track" refers to someone who works on a certain street or area selling sex in person, as opposed to people who are sold online for sex.

[30] This is information Douglas Gilmer gave at the National Trafficking Sheltered Alliance anti-trafficking conference in September 2020. All other references to Gilmer are from a personal interview unless otherwise noted.

[31] From the National Trafficking Sheltered Alliance conference.

[32] From the National Trafficking Sheltered Alliance conference.

[33] From the National Trafficking Sheltered Alliance conference.

[34] From the National Trafficking Sheltered Alliance conference.

[35] From the National Trafficking Sheltered Alliance conference.

[36] This is information Amy Wagar gave at the National Trafficking Sheltered Alliance anti-trafficking conference in September 2020. All other references to Wagar are from a personal interview and emails unless otherwise noted.

[37] MSSW is Master of Science in Social Work.

[38] From the National Trafficking Sheltered Alliance conference.

[39] From the National Trafficking Sheltered Alliance conference.

[40] From the National Trafficking Sheltered Alliance conference.

[41] BSW is a Bachelor of Social Work.

[42] LICSW is Licensed Independent Clinical Social Worker. Oden is also a Registered Nurse.

[43] M. Ed. is Master of Education.

INDEX

Gaming systems, 43, 50, 151
Gangs, 38-39, 73
GenerateHope, 75, 94
Gift(s), 29, 71, 93
Girls Educational and Mentoring Services (GEMS), 22, 87
Grace to Glory Counseling, 83
GraceHaven, 84, 147
Grindr, 52
Groom(ed)(ing), 28-29, 43, 52, 53, 69-71, 78, 89, 110
    Online, 43, 47, 48, 49, 53
GroupMe, 51
Guilt, 73

Handle, 53
Harboring, 109
Hashtags, 51
Healing, 147-51
Hinge, 52
Hippocampus, 98
Homeless(ness), 70, 84, 87
Hope, 34, 60, 119, 137, 141, 147, 147-51
Human rights, 8, 16
Human smuggling, 18
Human trafficking, 3, 4, 16-17, 18, 114, 121, 122, 123, 124, 125
    Child, 111
    Gang-related, 39
    Indigenous girls and women, 35
    Online, 48
    Page Act, 113
    TVPA, 108, 112, 117
    Victims, 5
Human Trafficking Prevention Project, 115
Hyperarousal, 96
Hypoxic, 96

Identity, 32
Identity disturbance, 89
Identity shift, 100
Implicit bias, 86, 102

SOURCES

Alicia Kozak. www.aliciakozak.com/aliciaslaw. Accessed 13 Sept. 2021.

Alicia Project. www.aliciaproject.org/about-alicia-kozakiewicz.html. Accessed 13 Sept. 2021.

Alicia Project. www.aliciaproject.org/internet-safety-tips.html. Accessed 13 Sept. 2021.

Alliance to End Slavery and Trafficking. endslaveryandtrafficking.org/summary-trafficking-victims-protection-act-tvpa-reauthorizations-fy-2017-2. Accessed 22 Sept. 2021.

"Allow States and Victims to Fight Online Sex Trafficking Act of 2017 [FOSTA]." *U.S. Government Publishing Office,* 11 April 2018, www.govinfo.gov/content/pkg/PLAW-115publ164/pdf/PLAW-115publ164.pdf.

Angela. (Human trafficking survivor. Not her real name.) Interview. Conducted by Melanie K. Patterson, 13 Sept. 2020. Additional emails and text messages.

Baedke, Audrey. "Serving LGBTQ+ Survivors." Sheltered Virtual Conference, National Trafficking Sheltered Alliance, 17 Sept. 2020, online. Additional emails.

Beams, Darren. Interview. Conducted by Melanie K. Patterson, 6 Jan. 2022. Additional emails.

Billings, Penny. Interview. Conducted by Melanie K. Patterson, 13 May 2020. Additional emails.

Buckley, Glen. Interview. Conducted by Melanie K. Patterson, 21 Oct. 2021.

Collier, Teresa. Interview. Conducted by Melanie K. Patterson, 6 July 2020. Additional emails and text messages.

Collier, Teresa. "Interviewing and Communicating with Survivors." Sheltered Virtual Conference, National Trafficking Sheltered Alliance, 16 September 2020, online.

Davis, Sill. "Serving LGBTQ+ Survivors." Sheltered Virtual Conference, National Trafficking Sheltered Alliance, 17 Sept. 2020, online.

Emerson, Jessica. "Restoring Justice for Trafficking Survivors: The Impact of Criminal Record Relief." Sheltered Virtual Conference, National Trafficking Sheltered Alliance, 16 Sept. 2020, online. Additional emails.

Fight The New Drug. fightthenewdrug.org/get-the-facts. Accessed 15 Sept. 2021.

Gillece, Joan, Dr. "Beyond the Behavior: Trauma-Informed Care for Survivors and Direct Service Providers." Sheltered Virtual Conference, National Trafficking Sheltered Alliance, 15 Sept. 2020, online. Additional emails.

Gilmer, Douglas. Interview. Conducted by Melanie Patterson, 28 July 2020. Additional emails.

Gilmer, Douglas. "Partnering with Law Enforcement." Sheltered Virtual Conference, National Trafficking Sheltered Alliance, 17 Sept. 2020, online.

Harrison, Michelle, Dr. "Trauma-Informed Tactics." Sheltered Virtual Conference, National Trafficking Sheltered Alliance, 16 Sept. 2020, online. Additional emails.

"How Porn Can Fuel Sex Trafficking." Fight the New Drug, fightthenewdrug.org/how-porn-can-fuel-sex-trafficking. Accessed 15 Sept. 2021.

Joy, Amy. "A Survival Story of Amy Joy." Making Connections Between Human Trafficking and Childhood Trauma, Interventions and Prevention, 16 April 2021, Daystar Church, Cullman, Alabama. Additional emails.

Joy, Amy. Human Trafficking 101: Stories, Stats, and Solutions. Self-published, 2020.

Kent, Brian. "Legal Responses: Using the Civil Court." Sheltered Virtual Conference, National Trafficking Sheltered Alliance, 17 Sept. 2020, online. Additional emails.

Lloyd, Rachel. Girls Like Us: Fighting for a World Where Girls are Not for Sale, an Activist Finds Her Calling and Heals Herself. 1st ed., Harper, 2011.

McNeal, Elisha. "Serving Minors: Sharing Lessons Learned." Sheltered Virtual Conference, National Trafficking Sheltered Alliance, 17 Sept. 2020, online. Additional emails.

Moloney, Anastasia. "Grooming is gateway to child sex trafficking as 'seducing' moves online." Reuters, 16 June 2018, www.reuters.com/article/us-global-trafficking-technology-youth-idUSKBN1JD00I.

Munsey, Susan. "Trauma-Informed, Trauma-Specific, Trauma-Integrated Care." Sheltered Virtual Conference, National Trafficking Sheltered Alliance, 16 Sept. 2020, online. Additional emails.

Oden, Connie. Interview. Conducted by Melanie K. Patterson, 12 Oct 2020. Additional emails and text messages.

Polaris. polarisproject.org. Accessed 15 Oct. 2021.

Polaris. polarisproject.org/2020-us-national-human-trafficking-hotline-statistics. Accessed 29 Jan. 2022.

Polaris. polarisproject.org/human-trafficking. Accessed 15 Oct. 2021.

Polaris. polarisproject.org/recognizing-human-trafficking-vulnerabilities-recruitment. Accessed 7 Oct. 2021.

Polaris. polarisproject.org/understanding-human-trafficking. Accessed 15 Oct. 2021.

Polaris. polarisproject.org/wp-content/uploads/2017/03/Typology-of-Modern-Slavery-Summary.pdf. Accessed 15 Oct. 2021.

Pinter, Dani, Esq. "Litigation as Activism." Sheltered Virtual Conference, National Trafficking Sheltered Alliance, 16 Sept. 2020, online. Additional emails.

Potter, Carolyn. Interview. Conducted by Melanie K. Patterson, 10 April 2020. Additional emails.

Potter, Carolyn. "Partnering with Law Enforcement." Sheltered Virtual Conference, National Trafficking Sheltered Alliance, 17 Sept. 2020, online.

Powell, Stephany, Dr. "Litigation as Activism." Sheltered Virtual Conference, National Trafficking Sheltered Alliance, 16 Sept. 2020, online. Additional emails.

Robb, Michael. "Tweens, Teens, and Phones: What Our 2019 Research Reveals." *Common Sense Media*, 29 Oct. 2019, www.commonsensemedia.org/blog/tweens-teens-and-phones-what-our-2019-research-reveals.

Rotondi, Jessica Pearce. "Before the Chinese Exclusion Act, This Anti-Immigrant Law Targeted Asian Women." *History*, 19 March 2021, www.history.com/news/chinese-immigration-page-act-women.

Shared Hope International. sharedhope.org/wp-content/uploads/2021/09/Apps_Fact_Sheet_9.16.21.pdf. Accessed 10 Nov 2021.

Simpkins-McClain, Shelia. "Empowering Survivors Without Re-Exploiting." Sheltered Virtual Conference, National Trafficking Sheltered Alliance, 15 Sept. 2020, online. Additional emails.

"SESTA/FOSTA Examination of Secondary Effects for Sex Workers Study Act." *U.S. Government Publishing Office*, 8 Jan. 2020, www.govinfo.gov/content/pkg/BILLS-116s3165is/pdf/BILLS-116s3165is.pdf.

Stickle, Wendy, et al. *Human Trafficking: A Comprehensive Exploration of Modern Day Slavery.* Sage Publications, Inc., 2020.

Taber, Jennifer. "Serving Minors: Sharing Lessons Learned." Sheltered Virtual Conference, National Trafficking Sheltered Alliance, 17 Sept. 2020, online. Additional emails.

"These 16 States Passed Resolutions Recognizing Porn As A Public Health Issue." *Fight The New Drug*, fightthenewdrug.org/here-are-the-states-that-have-passed-resolutions. Accessed 15 Sept. 2021.

Thomas, Rachel. "Identity Disturbance: Ending the Game." Sheltered Virtual Conference, National Trafficking Sheltered Alliance, 16 Sept. 2020, online. Additional emails.

Thompson, Lisa. "Why Prostitution Policy Matters in the Fight to End Sexual Exploitation." Sheltered Virtual Conference, National Trafficking Sheltered Alliance, 17 Sept. 2020, online.

"Trafficking in Persons Report 2021." *U.S. Department of State*, June 2021, www.state.gov/wp-content/uploads/2021/09/TIPR-GPA-upload-07222021.pdf.

"Victims of Trafficking And Violence Protection Act of 2000." *U.S. Congress*, 28 Oct. 2000, www.congress.gov/106/plaws/publ386/PLAW-106publ386.pdf.

Wagar, Amy. Interview. Conducted by Melanie K. Patterson, 10 June 2020. Meeting on 17 Feb. 2022. Additional emails and text messages.

Wagar, Amy. "Interviewing and Communicating with Survivors." Sheltered Virtual Conference, National Trafficking Sheltered Alliance, 16 Sept. 2020, online.

Wagar, Amy. "Partnering with Law Enforcement." Sheltered Virtual Conference, National Trafficking Sheltered Alliance, 17 Sept. 2020, online.

West, Carolyn, Dr. "Black Girl Interrupted: African American Girls and Commercial Sexual Exploitation." Sheltered Virtual Conference, National Trafficking Sheltered Alliance, 16 Sept. 2020, online.

Whitcomb, Dan. "Backpage chief pleads guilty, will cooperate in prostitution case." *Reuters*, 12 April 2018, www.reuters.com/article/us-usa-justice-backpage-idUSKBN1HK03I.

"Who Buys Sex? Understanding and Disrupting Illicit Market Demand." *Demand Abolition*, November 2018, www.demandabolition.org/wp-content/uploads/2019/07/Demand-Buyer-Report-July-2019.pdf.

"Why Today's Internet Porn Is Unlike Anything The World Has Ever Seen." *Fight The New Drug*, fightthenewdrug.org/why-todays-internet-porn-is-unlike-anything-the-world-has-ever-seen. Accessed 15 Sept. 2021.

"Why Porn Can Be Difficult To Quit." *Fight The New Drug*, fightthenewdrug.org/why-porn-can-be-difficult-to-quit. Accessed 15 Sept. 2021.

Wilson, Kathy. Interview. Conducted by Melanie K. Patterson, 14 May 2020. Additional emails and text messages.

Zarzaur, Greg. "Legal Responses: Using the Civil Court." Sheltered Virtual Conference, National Trafficking Sheltered Alliance, 17 Sept. 2020, online. Additional emails and phone call.

About the Author

After learning about the reality of human sex trafficking while working as a reporter, Melanie K. Patterson has done extensive research on sex trafficking, anti-trafficking organizations and Internet safety. She has a B.A. in Anthropology from the University of Alabama at Birmingham and studied History at the graduate level. She has almost twenty years of journalism experience at newspapers in Alabama and Colorado. Melanie served eight years as a U.S. Army Reserve journalist, where she completed assignments in France, El Salvador, Bosnia-Herzegovina and across the United States. Melanie lives in north Alabama with her family. Visit her at www.forgedinwords.com, www.melaniepattersonbooks.com and on LinkedIn, Facebook and Instagram.

www.ingramcontent.com/pod-product-compliance
Lightning Source LLC
Chambersburg PA
CBHW060040030426
42334CB00019B/2411